Barons
of the
Beltway

Barons

of the

Beltway

INSIDE THE PRINCELY WORLD OF OUR
WASHINGTON ELITE—
AND HOW TO OVERTHROW THEM

Michelle Fields

CROWN
FORUM
NEW YORK

Published in the United States by Crown Forum, an imprint of the Crown Publishing
Group, a division of Penguin Random House LLC, New York.
crownpublishing.com

CROWN FORUM with colophon is a registered trademark
of Penguin Random House LLC.

Library of Congress Cataloging-in-Publication Data
Names: Fields, Michelle, author.
Title: Barons of the Beltway : inside the princely world of our Washington elite–
and how to overthrow them / Michelle Fields.
Description: First edition. | New York : Crown Forum, 2016.
Identifiers: LCCN 2015038097| ISBN 9780553447552 | ISBN 9780553447569 (ebook)
Subjects: LCSH: Political culture–United States. | Political corruption–United
States. | Elite (Social sciences)–Political aspects–United States.
Classification: LCC JK1726 .F54 2016 | DDC 306.20973–dc23
LC record available at http://lccn.loc.gov/2015038097

ISBN 978-0-553-44755-2
eBook ISBN 978-0-553-44756-9

Printed in the United States of America

Book design by Jennifer Daddio
Jacket design: Tal Goretsky
Jacket images: (*Capitol*) toos / Getty Images; (*secret service agents, from left*) Mark
Wilson / Getty Images; Jewel Samad / Getty Images; Saul Loeb / Getty Images; (*man
exiting car*) Blend Images / Superstock; (*car*) © Drive Images / Alamy Stock Photo

10 9 8 7 6 5 4 3 2 1

First Edition

To my brother Michael, without whom this book wouldn't exist. Thank you for helping me find my passion.

CONTENTS

As a journalist, I tell stories. I wrote this book to tell the story of a political class that has lost its way and lost touch with the people it is supposed to serve. But as a professional, I never intended to—and never thought I would—actually become the story myself.

On March 8, 2016, all of that changed.

That evening, I was working for Breitbart News covering a Donald Trump campaign rally after the billionaire won the Republican primaries in Michigan and Mississippi. As Trump was leaving the rally, I leaned in to ask him a question about affirmative action. Before he had a chance to answer, someone whom I didn't see but was identified by a *Washington Post* reporter standing next to me as Trump's campaign manager, Corey Lewandowski, grabbed me by the arm and jerked me aside. I lost my balance and nearly fell to the ground.

That moment started a whirlwind I didn't ask for and didn't want, and a story that took on a life of its own. Trump and Lewandowski denied the incident ever occurred, despite video and eyewitness evidence and the obvious bruises on my arm. My employer, Breitbart News—an outlet known for being friendly to Trump—opted to offer only a tepid response. A number of people parted ways with Breitbart over the incident—including, eventually, me. As a journalist, I knew I couldn't work for an outlet that prized access to a particular figure over the safety of its own staff.

Eventually the furor over the story died down, and my life went somewhat back to normal—or at least what passes for normal in the crazy D.C. media world. The Trump campaign rolled on (with Lewandowski still at the helm) mostly unabated. I had to find a job and get this book ready to come out in a few months. But when I had time to really consider the arm-grabbing incident, I found that it reminded me of why I wrote this book in the first place: to make the case against entitlement.

The entrenched politicians, bureaucrats, and consultants I've written about are pulling a giant scam on the American people because they believe they are better than everyone else. They think living in D.C. entitles them to the car service, the free food, the taxpayer-funded trips, and all the other perks that they "deserve" for their proximity to power. And what's worse—they're getting away with it.

Trump's running his own scam, too. He has perpetuated a campaign that actively promotes violence against people it perceives as a threat—be they protesters or journalists.

Trump has even bragged that he could literally get away with murder: "I could stand in the middle of Fifth Avenue and shoot somebody," he proclaimed in Iowa, "and I wouldn't lose voters." If that's not entitlement, what is?

Trump's entitlement has been brought on by constant media coverage and his cynical demagoguery of peoples' real concerns. And here's where the scam comes in: Trump was supposed to be different. He tricked many, many good people into believing that he was "authentic," that he would "tell it like it is"–and these people were so sick of the political class that they bought it. But while Trump may not have been a politician himself, he was still very much a part of the elite system that's been running Washington for far too long. The billionaire has been an active political donor–mostly to Democrats–for decades.

Trump didn't pick just any Average Joe to run his campaign, either. He picked Corey Lewandowski, a longtime political operative whose credentials included a stint working for former Ohio representative Bob Ney, who was jailed in connection with the Jack Abramoff lobbying scandal. Lewandowski even wrote a letter to the judge to try to help his former boss get off easy, praising Ney as a "consummate professional" (professional what?) and his own "surrogate father." It's hard to find a more literal example of Washington criminal corruption than Lewandowski's own "surrogate father" Bob Ney.

And then there's Trump himself. I won't give the whole thing away, but I begin this book with a visit to the Palace of Versailles, and some thoughts about one of history's greatest expressions of vanity made me think about the Washington, D.C., of today. When you read the descriptions in the next few pages–"Gold molding. Gold statues. Gold engravings. Gold shields. Gold Greek gods. . . . Gold everywhere!"–who does that make you think of? All King Louis XIV was missing were some steaks, some vodka, an airline . . . you get the idea.

Were Donald Trump to show up in Washington as president of the United States (with Corey Lewandowski as his chief of staff), he would fit in perfectly with the Beltway culture–a culture that rewards hucksters, cynics, and egomaniacs who have long ago sold their souls for a shot at power and perks.

The Trump phenomenon is a reminder that the entitlement that drives the Beltway class is alive and well. It lives in people who call themselves liberals and in people who call themselves conservatives. It lives in people who prefer to think of themselves as "the establishment" as well as those who make a career of calling for the establishment's downfall. It's a reminder that the disease is only getting worse, and that we need to stop it once and for all.

–Michelle Fields

Barons

of the

Beltway

Rioters of Versailles

I f you've never stayed at a hostel in Europe, consider yourself lucky. The sheets' stains look like a topographical map, and the mattresses feel like they've been through a Sharknado. You feel like you need a shower after you take a shower. And the wannabe hippies sleeping in the Che and anarchist shirts on the half-dozen bunks around you smell and snore and make you yearn for the relative opulence of an American truck stop.

Don't get me wrong. For a girl from Los Angeles who had always dreamed of seeing the Paris of *The Pink Panther* and *Sabrina,* visiting the City of Light on a shoestring budget was better than not seeing it at all. And on that budget, a hostel was all I could afford.

After I spent several nights in Paris, the cranky Frenchman (is that redundant?) at the hostel's front desk suggested

I visit the Palace of Versailles. "It's beautiful!" he said in a thick accent. "You'll love the gardens, the gold, everything."

I usually avoid touring palaces when I'm abroad. I can take only so many rooms of fancy furniture. But after another night of hoping the bunk beds around me were free of pickpockets and head lice, I was in the mood for a bit of glitz and glitter. Besides, it was the Fourth of July. I figured the home of Louis XVI, whose support helped Americans win our Revolution, would be a fitting place to be on Independence Day. Little did I know at the time that what I would find at Versailles would make me think not of Philadelphia in 1776 but of Washington in 2014.

A fter a ten-mile train ride from Paris, I found myself staring at the most awe-inspiringly enormous building I have ever set eyes on. Other palaces are just big castles, but the Palace of Versailles is a zip code. Some of its rooms are a third of a mile away from other rooms. With white stone walls and 2,000 windows surrounding a massive courtyard, the palace is home to 67 staircases, 700 rooms, 1,250 fireplaces, 2,100 sculptures, 7,000 paintings, and 15,000 engravings. It held up to 20,000 residents. One of its rooms featured 578 mirrors. Another was so large it took 10,000 candles to light it.

I quickly learned that the story of Versailles began with France's first absolute monarch, Louis XIV, who reigned until his death in 1715. Conveniently enough, Louis believed that God Himself had appointed him king—which he took as a

mandate to invade any neighbor, commission any art, sleep
with any woman, and build the biggest darn palace in Europe.

Louis didn't care what it would cost to build Versailles.
(Estimates range up to $300 billion in today's dollars.) But
he did care how long it took. At the height of his building
mania, he pushed 40,000 workers to the breaking point, day
and night, despite a steady stream of fatal falls and other ac-
cidents caused by unsafe working conditions. As I walked
through the estate's perfectly manicured gardens and
groves, I read that Louis wasn't even willing to wait for trees
to grow. Instead, he uprooted fully grown trees from all over
France and brought them to a backyard that would feature
twelve miles of roads, twenty-seven miles of trellises, and
eighty miles of trees—some 200,000 total.

Louis wasn't in a hurry just to build Versailles. He was
impatient in all things. Visitors to Versailles can learn that
while the so-called Sun King waited for a love interest to dis-
robe, he would frequently have sex with her chambermaid,
before returning to the now sufficiently unclothed mistress.
Once the tryst ended, the mistress would go back to one of
twenty rooms in Versailles built for the king's lovers. (Louis
built "just" eleven rooms for his wife.)

No two rooms at Versailles capture Louis XIV's penchant
for exuberance, self-absorption, and utter excess better than
the Salon of War and the adjoining Hall of Mirrors. When
I walked into the former, it occurred to me that I was probably looking at more gold on its four-stories-tall walls than
on all the other walls I had ever seen in my life. Gold molding. Gold statues. Gold engravings. Gold shields. Gold Greek

gods. Gold borders dividing ceiling paintings of conquered European neighbors. Gold everywhere! Except in the center of one wall. There, below two gold angels blowing gold trumpets and above two gold prisoners in gold chains, is a plasterwork bas-relief of Louis XIV on horseback. He is trampling on his enemies.

The Salon of War is, however, a mere appetizer of opulence and narcissism compared to the room I walked into next. My first thought was "The Hall of Mirrors is aptly named." Eighty yards long and again four stories tall, its marble walls are covered by no less than 578 mirrors. They reflect light from 17 ornate windows that stretch to the gilded molding of the ceiling, and from three rows of 43 solid silver chandeliers, which in their heyday were lit by 3,000 candles. The arched ceiling is painted in Sistine Chapel style, but instead of celebrating God's creation of the universe, the images represent the glorious reign of Louis XIV.

As I walked through the most famous room in France, I stopped at one of its seventeen windows. Before me was the Grand Canal. It is so large that within its four-mile perimeter, the king liked to stage mock battles.

It occurred to me that Versailles was the perfect place for a fake battle, because there was something fake about a lot of Versailles. Its grounds include Marie Antoinette's make-believe "Queen's Hamlet," complete with a mock farmhouse, mock dairy, and mock poultry yard. With her entourage, the queen—wife of Louis XVI—would dress like a shepherdess, milk cows that had been washed and groomed by servants, and take lambs on silk leashes for walks through the gardens.

Across the Grand Canal from the Queen's Hamlet, the king indulged in his own bit of isolation from reality. All three kings who lived at Versailles liked to hunt on the estate's Grand Park. (Louis XIV reputedly hunted three times a day, made love three times a day, and held a meeting of his council three times a day.) But hunting at Versailles was unlike hunting in the rest of France, where hunters competed with wolves that preyed on deer and boar and that posed an acute threat to the hunters themselves. (Wolves ranked high, alongside bandits, on the list of causes of death in rural France.) Surrounding the Grand Park were large ditches called "wolf plunges." They formed a sort of moat that kept wolves away from the king's hunting grounds.

As I stood at the window in the Hall of Mirrors looking out toward the Queen's Hamlet to my right and the king's Grand Park to my left, I thought about all the other ways in which Versailles was more a facade than a reality. I had been to the Chapel Royal, where mass was once held daily. But outside of the chapel's walls was once a degree of vice and debauchery that would make even a Kennedy or a Clinton blush. Louis XV had at least fifteen illegitimate children, some born from orgies with teenage girls he kept at a brothel on royal grounds called the Deer Park.

If Versailles was a place where the queen pretended to be a shepherdess and the king pretended to be a virtuous Christian, it was also a place where nobles pretended to believe them. Louis XIV built Versailles in part to keep his nobles under control in one place, and, for a while, it worked. They fought for the bedroom closest to the king's, for the chair closest to his at the banquet table, and for the privilege every morning of being among the entourage of sycophants who helped the king and queen put on their clothes. The flattery reached such heights that when the king asked a noble when his wife was expecting to deliver their baby, the response was "When your majesty wishes it."

I thought back to my first impression of Versailles's size. Imagine being surrounded by five football fields of nobles, all from the same social class, all with the same vested interests in the status quo. It's no wonder that, after a while, the inmates started to run the asylum. When economic experts warned Louis XVI that his taxing and spending was driving the people deeper and deeper into poverty and hunger, the king rejected the advice. He backed away from a proposal that would have abolished a host of expensive, unnecessary jobs held by Versailles's courtiers. By then, the king was a pawn in the hands of the ruling class. Meanwhile, Versailles—one single palace!—was consuming up to 25 percent of the government's annual income.

In the end, the monarchs were not well served by the expensive bubble they built to isolate themselves from the harsh realities of their kingdom. While the royals and their court wined and dined their way through carefree days of hunting, staging mock battles, and leading sheep with silk leashes, their people were literally starving to death. At the time of the Revolution, France's national debt was the rough equivalent of $1.5 trillion today. Louis XVI tried (and failed) to spend his way out of debt—an early and disastrous attempt at a version of Keynesian economics.

When I reached Marie Antoinette's bedroom at Versailles, I looked for a while at the small, secret door she used to flee the mob bent on murdering her in 1789, when starving peasants broke down the gates of Versailles, stormed the palace, killed one of her guards, and called for her head. At first, I thought about how the queen must have felt. She was awoken from her bed by the shouting of the horde and the breaking of windows, doors, and anything else in the way of the rioters. She was face-to-face with people who wanted to kill her. Hungry people. Enraged people. As deadly as they were bedraggled. She must have been absolutely terrified—and not just for herself, but for her children as well.

But before I let myself sympathize too much with the queen, I tried to imagine what the rioters would have been thinking. They had long ago accepted the economic fate of their fathers—a lifetime of poverty with no hope for a better life. But they rebelled when even the small necessities of that life were taken from them—necessities such as bread, which had skyrocketing prices. Day after day, year after year, they worried, on empty stomachs, about whether they would find a way to feed themselves.

Most of the rioters were women, and they were painfully familiar with the hardest choices a mother can make. How much food do I give my children? How do I divide it among them? How much do I keep for myself? What rage they must have felt once they breached Versailles's gates and cast their eyes on the opulent waste of a government that clearly cared more about its own luxuries than about its people's welfare and survival.

After leaving the queen's bedchamber, I headed for the train and the ride back to Paris. But as I relaxed on the return trip, I couldn't get the image of Marie Antoinette's secret door out of my head. The royal family had built Versailles in part to isolate themselves from their subjects. Marie's secret door wasn't just any door—it was the entryway into another life. It led to private rooms, apartments, chambers, and hallways. When her favorite guests came to Versailles, this was where she would have them stay. The door was an added layer of isolation from the people. The door was a vessel further into her bubble.

Of course, in the end, the small door would provide her only the most temporary of escapes. Four years later, she lost her head to the guillotine.

For me, that door—and in a larger sense, all of Versailles—symbolizes that all bubbles must one day burst.

Louis XIV built a bubble at Versailles to isolate himself from his nation. At Versailles, there was no famine. At Versailles, there was no poverty. At Versailles, there was no one to criticize the king's poor policies, call him out on his moral hypocrisy, or contradict his belief that God Himself had made him France's king.

That isolation from reality was fun for the whole family—until Marie Antoinette heard the roar of the mob and looked in panic at her bedroom's hidden door. At that moment, the bubble burst. The consequences of the government's ruinous taxes and spending and rapidly mounting debt could no longer be ignored or wished away. There is only so much arrogance, corruption, and waste that any nation can endure.

• • •

I'm glad I visited Versailles, but not for the reason the cranky Frenchman thought I would enjoy it. For him, Versailles's opulence embodies the glory Louis XIV imagined when he built it. But for me, it was a cautionary tale that began with narcissism and ended in tragedy. Behind the facade of gold rooms and lavish decorations was a morally and fiscally corrupt court wasting the finances of a bankrupt country, surrounded on all sides by impoverished victims of the ruling class's arrogance and isolation. Does that sound familiar?

Versailles reminded me of another city composed of out-of-touch elites and government officials living lavishly off the taxpayers while regular citizens suffer under the crushing realities of a poor economy and heavy taxation.

In other words, it reminded me of the Beltway (Washington, D.C., and the wealthy suburbs in Maryland and Virginia that surround it).

Today in Washington, members of Congress who are elected to "represent" the American people enjoy opulent lifestyles. They make more than three and a half times the average household income, are provided with multiple offices, and, in the case of the Senate, even enjoy their own taxpayer-subsidized Senate Hair Care shop. They ride in their own elevators, travel on their own subway, and eat in their own dining room. During the recession, the average American's net worth dropped by 8 percent, while the average wealth of members of Congress increased by 15 percent.

Today in Washington, members of Congress routinely abuse their position of power to financially assist their free-loading relatives. Many of them pay family members through their PACs, campaigns, or congressional offices. They divert millions of dollars of federal contracts and earmarks to their children and siblings. And they send their campaign funds straight into their families' pocketbooks.

Today in Washington, members of Congress are chauf-feured to their Capitol Hill offices even when they live only two blocks away. And when it comes to foreign travel, the waste is even more pronounced. One out of every three members of Congress billed taxpayers for international travel to places such as Monaco and the French Riviera, often on military planes that cost taxpayers $10,000 per hour. The president's travel is even worse. His plane, Air Force One, costs taxpayers $206,000 per hour. When President Obama took it to Hawaii for vacation, the government charged taxpayers $134,000 for hotel rooms and $251,000 for police overtime.

Today in Washington, government agencies plan and throw lavish parties to celebrate themselves. For example, the General Services Administration threw a party where they spent thousands of dollars on a mind reader, more than $6,000 for commemorative coin sets, and $75,000 on a training exercise to build a bicycle. The Department of Justice spent $58 million in 2012 for conferences in Indonesia, Senegal, and the Northern Mariana Islands.

Today in Washington, some federal officials qualify for pensions after just five years of government work. Members of Congress who serve twenty years are eligible for a $59,000 pension at the age of fifty. Former presidents can receive over $1 million a year in pensions, benefits, "transition" funds, and other expenses—even though they make millions through their foundations, speaking engagements, corporate board memberships, consulting gigs, and book deals.

Today in Washington, members of Congress can acquire fortunes through sweetheart loans, insider trading, and diverting federal funds to boost the value of their land holdings. One used campaign funds to pay herself $228,000 in interest on a loan from her personal account to her campaign. Another sponsored an $18 million earmark for a bridge just a few miles from land he owned. Still others—along with their staff members—legally buy and sell stocks based on insider knowledge.

Today in Washington, members of Congress and their aides are exempted from many of the laws they write, including much of Obamacare, financial accounting laws, minimum wage laws, the Freedom of Information Act, collective bargaining laws, and workplace safety regulations that burden and sometimes bankrupt businesses.

Today in Washington, the president hands out cushy ambassadorships as thank-you gifts for donors' fundraising efforts. The more money someone gives, the higher the likelihood they will end up with one of the ritzier posts. Ambassadors and their aides live in embassies and sleep in lavish ambassador residences that can cost up to $1 billion to build. They can include indoor basketball courts, six-lane swimming pools, irrigated soccer fields, and (in London) a pond, park, and gardens on each floor.

In short, our nation's capital has become a modern Versailles—where arrogance and corrupt self-dealing are the norm, and where the governing class has completely lost touch with the governed.

Nothing better illustrates the dichotomy between the lives of the governing and the governed than the first few minutes after Senate Minority Leader Harry Reid walks out his door on a typical morning. As the Nevada Democrat steps out of the elevator and into the lobby of his luxury condominium at the Ritz-Carlton, a man dressed in a suit rushes to grab his laptop bag so that the senator doesn't have to hold it a second longer than necessary. The Ritz-Carlton bellhop knows not to call for taxi service or offer Reid directions to the closest metro station, because the senator's three black luxury SUVs, all paid for by the American taxpayer, are lined up in front of the Ritz, waiting for him, their engines idling. Reid's taxpayer-funded chauffeur immediately gets out of the car to open the door for him. Pedestrians walking by have no idea who Reid is, but the black luxury car tells them all they need to know—that he is powerful and important.

Indeed, the black SUV, equipped with red and blue WEG lights to ease its passengers through gridlocked Washington traffic, has become more than just a vehicle; it has become the status symbol of our nation's capital. The more of them you have traveling with you, the more power you have in Washington.

One of the first things Kwame Brown did when he was

elected chairman of the Council of the District of Columbia was to order a "fully loaded" Lincoln Navigator L with a power moonroof and aluminum wheels. He also requested that the interior and exterior be completely black. The cost for leasing the black luxury car for the chairman amounted to $1,900 a month. In 2011 alone, taxpayers footed the bill for D.C. mayor Vincent Gray's $1,941-a-month Navigator and another $1,785 for his security team. In 2014 then secretary of state Hillary Clinton committed a gaffe by admitting she hadn't driven herself since 1996–she lives a life inside a black SUV, too. President Obama has a fleet of Suburbans on hand, running through the night, on the off chance they might be needed for an emergency.

The vehicles used to chauffeur government officials like Clinton and Reid around are available day and night at the government officials' beck and call. The chauffeur drops the government official off wherever he or she requests and parks the vehicle outside the building or restaurant. The chauffeurs usually play games and surf the Internet on their phones to pass time. They wait for officials for hours on end, and all the while their engines are running.

Politicians like Reid regularly condemn the large SUVs that some of their constituents enjoy driving. In 2008 Reid hosted the National Clean Energy Summit in Las Vegas, where he blasted the large vehicles that Americans drive, arguing that using them "harms our economy, threatens our national security, and pollutes our environment."

But politicians like Harry Reid don't mind being driven in SUVs to and from the speeches they make condemning them. While they make these speeches purporting to care about the environment, their multiple-car motorcades idle in the parking lot releasing carbon dioxide, nitrogen oxide, and other harmful pollutants into the environment. While D.C. and many states have enacted anti-idling laws that the average American must abide by or pay a fine, government officials are able to idle for long periods of time without paying a penalty. The cost of having these luxury cars idling and needlessly burning fuel is of no importance to the government official or his chauffeur because, at the end of the day, it's the taxpayer who ends up footing the bill. Every member of Congress is currently eligible for a monthly $1,000 stipend to rent luxury vehicles to transport them to meetings, lunches, and wherever else they need to go.

The government owns 450,000 such civilian cars, which include the popular black Chevrolet Tahoe SUV. The Environmental Protection Agency is responsible for reducing pollution from gas-guzzling cars, but it maintains a stockpile of unnecessary cars that include luxury sedans such as Audis, BMWs, and Porsches. According to the Government Accountability Office, the federal government spends $3 billion annually on operating and maintaining its fleet.

The black luxury car has become the embodiment of everything America has grown to hate about Washington. It is also a tangible symbol of what's wrong with our federal government: Its leaders simply have no understanding of the basic needs and concerns of average Americans who pay for their own gas, drive their own cars, brave daily gridlock, and struggle to find parking places. No chauffeur waits patiently outside most Americans' houses for them, or grabs their briefcase, or hands them a crisp paper to read on a commute.

As a place to live, Washington, D.C., has a certain magnetism, and the reason is very clear—the high-paying government work. People don't flock to Washington for the weather. They migrate to D.C. because of an ever-growing market for people wanting to "serve the people."

It is no coincidence that four out of the five wealthiest counties in America are in the vicinity of Washington, D.C. While Americans have seen their average income decrease over the past decade by 6 percent, to $51,371, the income of the typical D.C. household increased by 23 percent between 2000 and 2012, to an inflation-adjusted $66,583. In the Washington metro area, the median household income is even higher, at $88,233.

Everywhere you look in Washington, there are new shops, restaurants, and luxury high-rise condos popping up. The population growth rate since 2010 has consistently been around 2 percent. The population growth is even spilling over to Virginia and Maryland, with Virginia's population growing by 0.9 percent, to 8.3 million, and Maryland's growing by 0.7 percent, to 5.9 percent. Unsurprisingly, the areas seeing the biggest boom are the counties bordering Washington, D.C., including Arlington County, Loudoun County, Montgomery County, and Prince George's County.

Like the Bourbons' Versailles, Washington is a hub for government parasites whose livelihoods depend on a bloated system of bureaucracy that must keep growing and growing. Like Versailles, it has never been a place people travel to in order to implement their innovative or entrepreneurial ideas. Like Versailles, it has never been a center for real commerce where entrepreneurs take actual risks. Like Versailles, Washington has a robust economy driven by the centralization and expansion of government.

Just how dependent is the city on the government? When the government shut down in October 2013, the cost to D.C.'s economy (including the Maryland and Virginia suburbs) in lost wages was $217 million per day. The city also lost $44 million per week in economic activity.

But aside from a couple weeks of a government shutdown, Washington is doing quite well. Due to the constant growth of the federal workforce, it was the only metropolitan area that escaped the long recession relatively unscathed. Just like Versailles, Washington grows more expansive and wealthier. All the while, Americans outside the Beltway continue to suffer under dreadful economic conditions caused in part by mistakes made by politicians in Washington who are living in their own little world.

That's what this book hopes to address—not just the shocking stories of daily governmental waste and abuse, but the serious detachment between our elected officials and reality. It looks at the hidden perks, the freebies, and the ego stroking that define life for a political class that is out of touch and out to lunch. The American people send public servants to Washington to represent them, but they live such lavish lives on the taxpayers' dime that it has become impossible for them to understand the everyday struggles of the American people.

In 2015, when discussing the power of the executive branch, the late Supreme Court justice Antonin Scalia declared that America has created a "presidency more reminiscent of George III than George Washington." Scalia's assessment was correct; we have an executive branch that's reminiscent of a monarchy. The office of the presidency has forgotten that we command him; he does not command us. So why is he treated like a king? Why is he received as a king? We are not his subjects. We are American citizens, and he is our servant.

And this problem isn't just limited to the presidency; this is about the entire government and all of Washington. The city has become one of the greatest threats to America's freedom since George III. We have to go to battle not with a man across the pond, but rather with an entire area in this country.

The Washington, D.C.-area population continues to boom for all the wrong reasons. It's not as if the Beltway is comparable to Silicon Valley, a hub for innovation. There isn't an innovative industry that continues to draw people into the area. Washington, D.C., is simply a hub for people who work for and live off the American monarchy. It's the taxpayers who ultimately sign the checks of most of the people in the Beltway, but D.C. folks spend their working hours trying to get in the good graces of those in the White House and on Capitol Hill. Their lives revolve around exchanging favors, attending fancy cocktail parties, networking, and seeking to rise a little higher on the ladder of power. They are isolated from normal American life and spend little time thinking about citizens outside the Beltway. The only time the average American comes to mind is when election season rolls around. That's when elected officials will leave their Brioni suits or Max Mara dresses in the closet, take out their jeans and T-shirts, attend events at diners and state fairs, and pretend that they're average Americans in order to maintain power. They then get reelected and go back to their taxpayer-funded bubble of luxury.

Our nation's capital was named after a man who embodied the most humble and democratic of our nation's principles. George Washington shocked the world by refusing a royal title and limiting his rule to two elected terms in office. He and his generation of Americans despised the trappings of royalty. After all, they had not fought a revolution against one king so that they could replace him with a different king. Nor did they pledge their "lives," "fortunes," and "sacred honor" to build nation with a ruling class of corrupt free-loaders and profiteers. We must ask ourselves whether we as a nation will demand better than the debt, taxes, and exorbitant spending that led to Marie Antoinette waking up in the middle of the night, turning her head in panic toward that small hidden door in the back of her bedchamber, and fleeing to escape the inevitable.

CHAPTER 1

An Era of Humility

I n 1774, our founding fathers fought to break away from a monarchy that no longer represented their interests. They were fed up with the excessive taxes, the pomp, and their distant ruler, King George III. After suffering at the hands of Great Britain, they led a revolution against the powerful empire and established the United States of America in 1776. It was to be a land in which all men were created equal.

This revolution was to be everlasting. It wasn't meant to end at the inception of America; rather, it was to live on with each American generation. To our founding fathers, being American was about possessing a democratic spirit–the spirit of '76. In their eyes, that spirit would become a part of what America is. It didn't matter if it was 1776 or 2016, Jefferson believed that the American spirit would open our eyes and motivate us to fight for the ideals that he and our forefathers risked their lives for.

And if we are to open our eyes, what we'll see is an America in dire need of the spirit of '76. Today, we have our own distant power abusing the American people. We aren't being abused from across the pond, but rather across the Potomac. The city that was named after George Washington no longer resembles the ideals that the man, or our other founding fathers, represented. Currently, Washington, D.C., looks more like a city King Louis XVI and Marie Antoinette would have loved rather than the city our founding fathers envisioned and fought to create.

Our founding fathers not only formed an independent nation but also created an entirely new frame of mind. They embraced and exuded one of America's founding virtues: humility. They were ambitious and strove for greatness for America, but were stripped of the pretentiousness of European monarchs. They disliked the ostentation of the royals and worked hard to eliminate the manners and thinking that characterized aristocratic society in Europe. But the norms and behaviors that our founding fathers worked so hard to eradicate have slowly found their way back into Washington's bloodstream. We are now living in an era of a power-hungry class obsessed with self-promotion and wealth. And we are working to promote them. Many in society continue to reinforce the arrogant over the humble—we've created the Kardashians, for goodness' sake! In the workplace, it's the brazen employee who gets promoted, not the humble employee who deflects credit for success. In politics, it's the arrogant politicians who keep getting elected. Arrogance has reached epidemic proportions. It's poisoning the American character and it's about time we work to rein it in.

A Country Steeped in Humility

"What do you do?" may be the number one question asked in the Beltway. It achieves two things: It gives the asker the opportunity to brag about their own job title and lets them know whether the person they're talking to is worth their time.

Job titles and associations are the lifeblood of D.C. You're no one unless you have a title, whether it's "congressman," "ambassador," "chief of staff," or an impressive title at a firm or media company. Unlike most jobholders in America, politicians in D.C. get to keep their titles for life. Think about it: You can be the CEO or vice president of the largest corporation in America, but once you leave that job, so goes the title. In Washington, D.C., you can have the title of "president," "congressperson," or "senator," and that is your title for life. It doesn't matter if you were a terrible congressperson who served only one term; you will forever be referred to and introduced as a "congressperson."

It's bizarre perks of D.C. power like this that draw thousands of young, type-A recent college grads to Washington—out of a desire not to serve our country but to get a title. And if you don't have a title, good luck getting someone to talk to you for longer than two minutes. Washington is a town obsessed with titles and where being an obnoxious blowhard is socially acceptable. But it wasn't always like this, and it's certainly not what our founding fathers envisioned.

When President Thomas Jefferson held parties, he refused to use his title. In his eyes, titles were the obsession of monarchies, not of democratic nations. So he would send out invitations to official engagements using his own name rather than "president."[1] He replaced bowing with the shaking of the hand.

And the dinners thrown by our founding fathers didn't include them wearing $12,000 garments or eating with gold cutlery like our public officials today. They understood their important role in setting a precedent for future generations and their role in conveying to the world the ideals of their young country. They did everything they could to distance themselves from the opulent lifestyles reminiscent of a monarchy. Jefferson proudly wrote in 1802 that he and the founding fathers "have suppressed all those public forms and ceremonies which tended to familiarize the public eye to the harbingers of another form of government."[2]

Jefferson wanted to ensure that the pomp and show of European courts was eliminated during dinnertime, and that instead the simplicity and informality of America were represented. He would wear austere clothing that he believed best reflected rural values. And when it came time for parties and social functions, Jefferson would go out of his way to ignore the aristocratic protocols of his former country. He insisted that round tables be used at dinners in order to project the democratic spirit of America. He didn't like the rectangular tables used at royal functions, which would seat guests according to their rank and status. Jefferson figured that, at a round table, no one could sit at the head and no one could mistake him for a king.[3] He believed that "when brought together in society, all are perfectly equal, whether foreign or domestic, titled or untitled, in or out of office."[4]

When the British minister to the United States, Anthony Merry, and his wife paid a visit to President Jefferson's White House, Secretary of State James Madison accompanied them. The Merrys were excited and arrived wearing their finest clothing for the exciting introduction. Mr. Merry was in full diplomatic dress, even wearing a ceremonial sword and gold braid.[5] But when they arrived at the main hall in the residence, they were flabbergasted—where was President Jefferson? The couple was accustomed to royal protocol, which said that the president ought to be waiting for them in the reception room. They stood there impatiently, but Jefferson was nowhere to be found.

Since Jefferson wasn't there, James Madison went to look for him with Mr. Merry. As they were walking through a passageway, Jefferson popped out of his study and greeted them. Merry was shocked—appalled. Not only did the president break protocol by failing to greet them upon their arrival, but he also wasn't even dressed for the occasion! Merry, dressed in his ceremonial sword and lavish outfit, felt ridiculous standing in front of President Jefferson, who was dressed casually in unceremonious workday clothing and wearing slippers.

According to Merry, the president of the United States

was "not merely in an undress but actually standing in slippers down at the heels, and both pantaloons, coat, and under-clothes indicative of utter slovenliness and indifference to appearances, and in a state of negligence actually studied."[6] The Merrys assumed that Jefferson's informality had to be a mistake. They thought that maybe they had just caught President Jefferson at a bad time. He must have been utterly embarrassed. But Jefferson's casualness was deliberate. His relaxed style was meant to send a message to his foreign guests: America was different. It was not meant to be a personal insult to Merry. It was meant to send a message to Great Britain about America's values.

A few days later, the Merrys were invited back to the White House for an official dinner. They were told to meet for a reception in the drawing room before dinner. They were hesitant to return but accepted the invitation under the assumption that they would likely be the guests of honor and treated exceptionally well as an apology for the embarrassing incident earlier. As they waited in the drawing room they figured that President Jefferson would arrive and apologize profusely. Jefferson did no such thing.

Jefferson arrived when it was time for dinner. Rules of protocol were such that Jefferson was supposed to take the arm of Mrs. Merry and escort her to the table. Instead, Jefferson took the arm of Dolley Madison, who served as the White House hostess for the widowed Jefferson. Jefferson escorted Madison to the table and ignored the shocked Mrs. Merry. Mr. Merry was furious to say the least. What kind of country was this man running?

To make matters worse, when the Merrys arrived at the dinner table they realized that there wasn't a seat designated for them. They figured there must be a mistake. The Merrys were accustomed to attending events where they were seated according to their rank. However, Jefferson's seating arrangement was pell-mell. It was a first-come, first-served arrangement, so all guests were seated according to how quickly they sat at the table. Mr. Merry was forced to scramble and compete for seats with other, inferior guests.

The Merrys viewed Jefferson's irreverence toward foreign dignitaries—and others accustomed to royal treatment—as insulting. But Jefferson felt that the informality was necessary. He wanted to send a clear message that America was democratic and that he wasn't going to carry on the arbitrary rules and protocol that dictated royal life. He didn't care if Merry had some fancy title. He wanted to show the couple that in America royal titles would be obsolete and all would be treated equal. One doesn't get a good seat simply because one has a title.

The Almost King

George Washington had the opportunity to seize absolute power and become king. And he had this opportunity not once, but twice.

After Washington had won the decisive battle at Yorktown, he had the chance and the support to establish an American monarchy. Congress had given Washington such wide-ranging powers during the war that it would have been

quite simple and likely tempting to transition into a dicta-
tor. Also, there reportedly were whisperings among officers
that Washington should be king. Many of his men were convinced that he had to become king. They felt that he was in-
dispensible and that America needed him in absolute power
in order for the country to survive.

With rumors swirling and clandestine support from soldiers, Washington had to make the decision. He had absolute
power at his fingertips—he just needed to decide whether it
was what he wanted. The world awaited in anticipation for
Washington's response.

King George III, curious of the decision Washington
would make, asked his American painter, Benjamin West,
what Washington was going to do after the Revolution. West
told the king that "they say he will return to his farm."[7] King
George III was shocked—how could a man seriously consider
turning down the chance of becoming king?

The king was later heard saying that if Washington would
really step aside, like he promised, then Washington would
be "the greatest man in the world."[8] And on December 23,
1783, in what is arguably one of the most important acts in
American history, George Washington entered the Maryland State House and addressed the president of the Continental Congress, Thomas Mifflin:

> Mr. President, the great events on which my resignation
> depended, having at length taken place, I have now the
> honor of offering my sincere congratulations to Congress
> and of presenting myself before them, to surrender into

their hands the trust committed to me, and to claim the in-
dulgence of retiring from the Service of my Country. . . .
Having now finished the work assigned me, I retire from
the great theatre of Action,–and bidding an affectionate
farewell to this August body, under whose orders I have so
long acted, I here offer my Commission, and take my leave
of all the employments of public life.[9]

The resignation was a reflection of how dedicated Washington was to republicanism. He retired to Mount Vernon
and swore off a public life. He wanted a humble and private
life. He returned to managing the estate and working on
the farm.

Then the nation called upon him to serve as president.
They were looking for one unifying national figure who was
a strong leader. There was no question; the man for the job
was America's national hero, George Washington. He had
gained the public's respect and showed his abilities by leading
the Continental Army through the war. And, during his time
as general, he had gained the love of soldiers throughout the
country. But Washington was cautious about reentering public life and was quite possibly America's most reluctant president. Unlike politicians today, George Washington didn't see
political life as a ticket to becoming wealthy and living off the
backs of taxpayers. He viewed public service for what it was
and ought to be: sacrifice and hard work. Similarly, he understood the gravity of the responsibility of leading such a young
nation. He also was a humble man who was honest with himself about what he perceived to be his shortcomings.

He wrote to Henry Knox, a military officer in the Continental Army, expressing his anxieties about the monumental position that was before him: "My movements to the chair of Government will be accompanied by feelings not unlike those of a culprit who is going to the place of his execution: so unwilling am I, in the evening of a life nearly consumed in public cares, to quit a peaceful abode for an Ocean of difficulties, without that competency of political skill, abilities and inclination which is necessary to manage the helm."[10]

He carefully weighed the decision. It seemed as though everyone in the country wanted him to be president except George himself. But he realized that the country needed him, and in 1789 George Washington was elected president. He became the first and last president in history to be elected unanimously.

Once president, Washington, like so many of our founding fathers, possessed immense humility, which complimented the democratic spirit of America. He was careful to appear as modest as possible in order to reflect the ideals of the young country. So when the question of what to call him arose, Washington chose a simple title.

Americans were used to referring to him as "General," but he needed a new title for his new position. Adams suggested calling Washington "Your Highness"–an honorific that today's politicians would kill for. But Washington settled for a less pretentious title, "Mr. President."

When he was inaugurated on April 30, 1789, Washington made sure to dress modestly, so that there would be no resemblance to the European royals. But his journey from Mount Vernon to New York for the inauguration proved difficult. In every city he stopped in, he was treated like a king, with church bells ringing and Americans lining up to catch a glimpse of him. The journey was like a coronation. By the time he arrived in Philadelphia to cheering crowds, he had become irritated with the royal treatment. Washington realized that the way he allowed others to treat him and the office would set a precedent for America. He didn't believe that the president should be shown such royal-like attention and admiration. Washington stayed in Philadelphia to rest, but according to a local paper, he left the city much earlier than planned in order to "avoid even the appearance of pomp or vain parade." When he made it to New York for the inauguration he chose to wear a suit made in America out of simple broadcloth.

During his time in office, he made sure not to isolate himself from the people he represented. He didn't want to appear as a detached monarch, so he had set days and times when constituents could come and speak to him about their concerns.

After his first term, Washington wrote to James Madison, then a congressional leader and close confidant, asking for help in putting together a farewell address. Madison obliged and composed a draft. But Madison and others convinced Washington to serve just one more term. They argued that the country would fall apart without him. Washington reluctantly agreed to serve a second term.

But once he completed the second term, Washington sent Alexander Hamilton, then the secretary of the Treasury, the farewell draft that Madison had written in 1792. He wanted him to look over the draft. Hamilton, like so many, didn't want Washington to deny a third term. But Hamilton obliged and edited the draft. On September 19, 1796, the farewell address was published in the *American Daily Advertiser.*

Washington's humility and leadership remind us of the gap between where America is and where it should be. He surrendered his power and sent a powerful message to the world and to future American generations. Washington could have been like Julius Caesar, Lenin, and other leaders before and after him who were loved by their people and used their popularity to remain in power until their deaths. However, Washington was, as King George said, "the greatest man in the world." It's no wonder that Washington, D.C., was named after him.

But the city that was named after one of the most admirable statesmen in history no longer resembles the ideals of the man. George Washington was a public servant; he never assumed the role of ruler. But today the city is infested with power-hungry politicians, not statesmen. The difference is that statesmen, like Washington, are called to service, whereas politicians enter public service to serve themselves. Our politicians don't have a humble bone in their bodies. They drive into D.C. each day, passing the monuments dedicated to our forefathers with one thing in mind: enriching themselves. While Americans work tirelessly each day to make a living and create value, our public servants are using your tax dollars to undo the work of the brave and virtuous public servants before them.

The Ambassador Has Cheap Clothes

In October 1776, Benjamin Franklin set sail for France as America's first ambassador. He was heading to a country that was the antithesis of America, and he had two critical tasks ahead of him: to generate support and money for America and to secure an alliance with France.

At the time, Franklin was arguably the most famous man in America. He had accumulated considerable wealth through printing and was able to afford to dress himself in the finest clothing—which he did. He also had quite the ego. "Humility" wasn't a word usually associated with Franklin, nor did it come naturally to him. But Franklin understood his role in the founding of America and the crafting of America's image.

So when he arrived in France, the French were shocked to see him show up in an unfashionable coonskin cap without a wig or a powdered nose.[11] His manner of dress was unseemly to the French. Even when he attended France's most lavish and fashionable royal events, he didn't wear expensive silk clothing or a uniform. Instead, he often opted for a modest brown suit.[12] He wanted to visibly display the difference between his America and Louis and Marie's France.

Madame Campan, who was the first lady-in-waiting to

Marie Antoinette, wrote about Franklin's appearance jux-
taposed with the diplomats at Versailles: "His straight un-
powdered hair, his round hat, his brown cloth coat, formed
a singular contrast with the laced and embroidered coats,
and powdered and perfumed heads, of the courtiers of Versailles."[13]

Because the French were fed up with the opulent lifestyle
of Marie and King Louis, they saw Franklin's radical fashion
sense as refreshing. The French found the novel idea of such
a wealthy and intelligent person dressing so soberly intrigu-
ing. Franklin was a hit in France.

He was revered across the country, and his likeness was
painted by artists and sold in shops throughout France. His
image appeared on watches and medallions.[14] French women
even began to imitate Franklin's soft fur cap by wearing a
wig resembling it, which became known as the *coiffure à la
Franklin.*[15] The French loved him and, by extension, America. In the eyes of average citizens in France, Franklin was
the embodiment of the country that they craved. He was the
personification of the spirit of a democratic America—of the
new frontier.

On the surface, his rustic and rural clothing may seem
to have been superficial or just a quirk. But his garments,
and the image of America that he projected, played an imperative role in securing an alliance with France during the
American Revolutionary War. Granted, Franklin's excep-
tional diplomatic skills, as well as the Americans' success
at Saratoga, helped sway France to recognize America and
form an alliance. But the French threw their support to the

fledgling country largely because of what America stood for and how America's public servants, specifically the humble Franklin, carried themselves.

The founders were dedicated to promoting democratic principles and knew that they were stewards in the grand experiment that was America. Benjamin Franklin, like our other forefathers, truly viewed himself as a public servant and held America's interests above his. It was their democratic spirit that helped America achieve greatness.

This desire to represent a humble and democratic country no longer exists in Washington. Take, for example, our former U.S. ambassador to France, Charles Rivkin, and his wife, Susan Tolson. They had "closet fairies" who ensured they didn't wear the same expensive designer outfit more than twice. Tolson confessed: "I've had to do more shopping to broaden my repertoire because I do think it's noticed if you wear the same thing more than twice or three times." She added, "Sometimes I'm changing clothes three times a day." Tolson dressed in designer gowns that cost as much as many Americans' cars. She dressed in the best labels: usually Michael Kors during the daytime and Christian Dior or Dolce & Gabbana in the evening.[16] She and her husband had a staff of thirteen people at their residence. When they went to Paris fashion shows in their pricey designer clothing, they were driven in armored cars with a six-person detail to secure them.[17]

No longer are our ambassadors concerned with possessing humility and strength—the central ingredients for good statesmen. Instead, our ambassadors are using public positions to live like royals. We are being represented by a class of narcissists whose pride is holding us back from being the great nation founded by our forefathers.

Humble Abe

In 1855, Abraham Lincoln was a forty-six-year-old attorney struggling for money. His political career hadn't taken off and he was looking for something to help pay off his accumulating debt. He was demoralized. He had seen himself as someone who would have a flourishing career by this point, but things just hadn't worked out. He was in search of a career breakthrough.

Then he received an offer from a firm that wanted him to take on a case involving two large Illinois companies that made reapers, the Cyrus McCormick Company of Chicago and the Manny Company of Rockford. The dispute between the two companies was over a patent. The Manny Company had hired three lawyers to represent it: George Harding, the well-known Edwin M. Stanton, and P. H. Watson.[18] But John H. Manny also wanted a lawyer located in the area of the trial–Springfield, Illinois. He didn't want to spend a lot of money, so he reached out to Lincoln, who was based in Springfield, and hired him. Lincoln was ecstatic–he received a $500 advance. Even more exciting was the fact that this was a high-profile case. Lincoln saw this as an opportunity. It didn't matter to him that he knew little about reapers. He would work hard and knock this case out of the park. This was his moment. He went straight to work on his oral

arguments, working diligently and even paying a visit to the
Manny factory in Rockford.

He worked on the case for months. During that time Lincoln reached out to Manny's other counsel to ask for updates.
But he never heard back. That didn't stop Lincoln; he kept
working. Then he heard that the trial was being moved from
Springfield to Cincinnati, Ohio. He decided to follow up
again with Manny's other counsel to finalize the details. On
September 1, 1855, he wrote:

> *Since I left Chicago about the 18th of July, I have heard*
> *nothing concerning the Reaper suit. I addressed a letter to*
> *Mr. Watson, at Washington, requesting him to forward me*
> *the evidence, from time to time, as it should be taken, but I*
> *have received no answer from him.*
>
> *Is it still the understanding that the case is to be heard at*
> *Cincinnati on the 20th inst.?*
>
> *Please write me on the receipt of this. Yours truly,*
>
> *A. LINCOLN.*

They didn't respond to Lincoln's letter. The truth was that
they didn't want Lincoln anymore. The trial had been moved
from Springfield to Cincinnati, so they saw no use for him.
The sole reason Lincoln was hired was simply because he was
from Springfield. Plus, they had the well-known and more intelligent legal mind of Edwin Stanton to take on the case. But
poor Lincoln was unaware of all of this. So when it came time
for the trial, he put on his best suit and headed to Cincinnati
to give his oral arguments.

When Lincoln arrived for the trial, Edwin Stanton and the rest of the legal team were disgusted by his homely appearance. Stanton described him as a "long, lank creature from Illinois, wearing a dirty linen duster for a coat[, on] the back of which perspiration had splotched wide stains that resembled a map of the continent."[19]

Lincoln was told that he was off the case. Nonetheless, Lincoln suggested that they all go into the courtroom together, but Stanton made it clear that he didn't want anyone to think he was associated with Lincoln. Stanton was overheard saying: "I will not associate with such a damned gawky, long armed ape as that."[20] Lincoln, who heard Stanton's comments, was understandably hurt. But he wanted to help the case, so he gave his oral arguments to the legal team to look at and use. They didn't even bother to read the work that Lincoln had spent the past few months preparing.

Although Lincoln was no longer on the case, he decided to stay in Cincinnati to hear the oral arguments. Often the lawyers would go out to eat and socialize. Lincoln never received an invitation. After the trip he wrote a friend from Cincinnati about his time there and said: "In reply to your request for me to come again I must say to you I never expect to be in Cincinnati again. I have nothing against the city, but things have so happened here as to make it undesirable for me ever to return here."[21] It was a difficult situation for Lincoln. He was angry at the circumstances and how Edwin Stanton had treated him. But it humbled him and motivated him to work harder.

Fast-forward six years: Lincoln is no longer some circuit

lawyer unworthy of representing a legal client alongside Edwin Stanton. Lincoln is now President Lincoln.

He was elected in 1860, and it was now time for him to assemble his team of advisers. Most politicians today immediately choose their staff from their tight-knit circle. These staffers usually agree with them on almost all major policy issues and have proven their loyalty and trustworthiness through their hard work on the campaign trail. But Abraham Lincoln was different. President Lincoln wasn't interested in who would best serve him. Rather, he was interested in those who would best serve his country during what was arguably the most difficult moment in America's history.

Lincoln, in a shocking move, chose his enemies for his cabinet. He realized that some of the most talented people in America were individuals who had competed with him for the presidency. He hired the other candidates for the Republican presidential nomination: Ohio governor Salmon P. Chase, New York senator William H. Seward, and the distinguished Missouri statesman Edward Bates. Filling up one's executive cabinet with enemies was unprecedented and is still unheard-of today. But Lincoln didn't care if he had bad blood with some of these people. He knew they were talented and would serve the country well—and that was his number one priority.

But in his first year as president, a problem arose with his secretary of war, Simon Cameron. Cameron was grossly incompetent and was dealing with rumors of corruption. Meanwhile, the Civil War was in its first year and Northern troops were losing battles. The Union was in trouble. What Lincoln needed was a bright and organized man at the helm. Lincoln knew it, and so did his old legal rival from Cincinnati—Edwin Stanton.

Since their last encounter in the courtroom in Cincinnati, Stanton had become one of the country's most impressive legal minds, and one of Lincoln's biggest critics. Stanton complained often about Lincoln's actions at the start of the Civil War, saying, "There is no settled principle or line of action—no token of any intelligent understanding by Lincoln."[22]

Today, American politicians would either ignore or seek vengeance upon those who viciously critique them like Stanton had done to Lincoln. But Lincoln was willing to put aside the personal offense and recognize Stanton's talents. He swallowed his pride and did what he thought was best for America: He appointed Stanton secretary of war. He didn't choose someone who would help him politically or someone who would be loyal to him; he chose the person he thought would help preserve the Union. He put America's interests above his, something that has become a rarity among our elected officials in Washington today.

Shortly after Stanton started his new position as secretary of war, Lincoln issued an authorization to his department. Stanton didn't agree with the president; he refused to carry out the authorization and said that Lincoln was a fool for issuing it. President Lincoln asked a member of Congress who was there: "Did Stanton say I was a damn fool?" The congressman said: "He did, sir, and repeated it." Most of the egocentric government officials today would likely call up the secretary of war and reprimand him. Not only did Stanton disobey an order given by the commander in chief, but he also insulted him. Instead, Lincoln put aside his ego and told the congressman, "If Stanton said I was a damn fool, then I must be one, for he is nearly always right and generally says what he means."[23]

It was Lincoln's humility and his deep commitment to America that allowed him to foster a good relationship with the man best fit for the job. And this special relationship helped preserve the Union. Lincoln's commitment to public service is what helped him put aside his insecurities and build the best cabinet he could, at one of the most critical moments in our history.

CHAPTER 2

The Perks of Being in Power

By the time our train arrived at Washington's Union Station, my day had already gotten off to a bad start. I had a busy day ahead of me, time was of the essence, and the train had been delayed for a while in New York City. Now there I was at Union Station, my final destination, wondering why we weren't allowed to get out of the train.

All of us had our bags in hand, ready to dart out the door. But then, with no explanation, a voice on the loudspeaker told us we had to stay inside the train. Groans could be heard from passengers as frustrated as I was.

About ten minutes later, as commuters texted their loved ones and business associates to explain why they were all going to be late, I saw a group of men with black suits and earpieces walking past our windows. What was going on? Did something bad happen?

After a further delay, the men in black walked past our car

again, headed back to their black SUVs. But this time, something was different. There was an older man in a sharp suit with horrible hair and a big, goofy grin. It was Vice President Joe Biden.

Suddenly, the reason for all the delays was obvious. But Biden seemed perfectly oblivious to the frustration and inconvenience he had caused hundreds of passengers. In fact, his demeanor suggested an assumption that we considered his presence an honor—maybe even a blessing.

How else to explain why he treated his walk down the platform like a cross between a papal audience and the Miss America pageant? His arm was extended out in a ninety-degree angle as he waved it with a subtle twist, as if he were a beauty queen sitting atop a float in the Thanksgiving Day parade. He smiled at all the passengers trapped in the Amtrak. Apparently, in his mind, all of us on the train were akin to Justin Bieber fans waiting for the pop star to exit the building so that we could catch a glimpse of him. Meanwhile, audible groans and "oh God" could be heard from the inside the train of delayed commuters late for their appointments, meetings, family, and friends.

Vice President Biden, like so many other politicians, has an inflated sense of importance. He believes that he is so great and that he's doing Americans a favor by gracing us with his presence. For such politicians, the idea that someone couldn't care less about being around them is a foreign idea that doesn't even cross their mind. They live in a bubble of their creation, filled with perks they've provided themselves–from special treatment on the Amtrak, to motorcades zipping through traffic, ritzy gyms, free vacations, PAC-funded parties, wasteful conferences, and air travel far more convenient than anything their constituents will ever experience. These are the trappings of political office that have created our founding fathers' worst nightmare–an American royal class.

This chapter pulls back the curtain on every one of these perks of power.

Hey, Joe, Where's the Fire?

A week after I saw our grinning buffoon of a vice president gliding by our delayed train, Biden's motorcade whizzed through traffic on the way to Georgetown, creating bottlenecks throughout the D.C. area as drivers were forced to stop their cars to let Biden's parade of black sedans and SUVs fly by.

Judging by the speed of his motorcade and the traffic it has caused, you would guess he was headed to an important meeting or briefing. But that's only if you don't know the ways of the elite in Washington, D.C., because Biden was, in fact, merely heading to the upscale Italian restaurant in Georgetown called Cafe Milano.

The Italian eatery is well-known in Washington for its clientele. It's the place that many Washingtonians go to dine when they want to be seen. It's a pricey one at that. A beef entrée can run you up to $200.

Biden and his wife, Jill, entered Cafe Milano and decided to sit outside at a table alongside the sidewalk. The vice president sat in the chair facing the street, deliberately trying to make eye contact with pedestrians in an attempt to be noticed. He was striking up conversation with anyone who walked by and noticed him. All the while, men in black suits stood on the sidewalk keeping a close eye on him, as their SUVs idled behind them.

When dinner ended, the vice president and his wife jumped back into the black SUV waiting for them. Several police cars drove before and behind him, whizzing at high speeds through Washington, D.C. Once again, hundreds of average Americans were delayed while Joe Biden was escorted in his train of vehicles in an emergency-like manner, as if the White House were on fire and Joe Biden were the fire marshal.

While it's clearly important to provide protection for our high-ranking officials in Washington, there comes a point where it's just excessive and a complete waste of our tax dollars. It's a whole lot of pomp and ceremony just to get an Italian dinner, but it shows what has become of our public servants. They don't care about the traffic congestion they cause for average Americans who are already stuck in terrible rush hour traffic. Why can't he sit in traffic with his protected vehicle? Why disrupt Americans' lives for an expensive plate of pasta? The answer is that they believe they deserve it and that the "little people," meaning all you average Americans, don't matter to them. They're clearly indifferent to the struggles of the average American and think that their meal is more important than you getting home in time for your dinner with your family. When Biden went to a private event in Colorado in September 2014, he took a forty-car motorcade. Biden doesn't care about the headache that road closures and a forty-car motorcade may cause you. Because he's Joe Biden.

Members of Congress aren't given a forty-car motorcade like Biden, but they are certainly not deprived of car perks. Each member of Congress is given the ability to spend $1,000 a month of our tax dollars on a luxury car and gas. Some members choose to use the $1,000 to lease BMWs or Mercedes-Benzes, or use the money to be driven around in black luxury cars.

So while Americans are just starting to recover from the Great Recession, their tax dollars are being used to chauffeur their public servants. Every American has to pay for his or her own car, as well as for gas, so why should it be any different for members of Congress? It isn't as if they are hurting financially. Most members of Congress have an average net worth of $1 million, clearly far wealthier than the average American.[1] So why is the average American paying for their car service?

The Secret Swimming Pool

The preferential treatment given to the vice president extends to Capitol Hill, and there's no better example of it than the congressional gym.

In June 2011, TMZ released images of the then congressman Anthony Weiner in a semi-nude pose. The photos of the congressman were taken in front of a mirror, with a towel wrapped around him. The married Democratic congressman had sent the photos to a young woman who was not wife.

In the background of the photos were lockers and a water cooler. The photos had been taken in the exclusive congressional "wellness center."

The photos had people scratching their heads and asking themselves: "Why on earth would he take this photo?" And: "Wait . . . Congress has its own gym?"

It would take a team of psychiatrists to answer that first question. But the answer to the second is simple: Yes, and you're paying for it!

If you go to the level below the basement of the Rayburn House Office Building and walk down a bland hallway, you'll pass two steel doors. The doors give no indication that behind them is a semi-secret gym where only members of Congress—and, of course, former members, because politicians like their perks to last for life—may work out. The gym has laundry service, workout machines, flat-screen televisions, a basketball court, and even a heated swimming pool.

How much does the gym, where members take half-naked selfies, cost? Well, that depends on whether you're wondering about the cost to legislators or the cost to you, the American taxpayer. House members pay only $20 a month for the gym. But the cost of maintaining it undoubtedly exceeds the amount of money members pay. Taxpayers cover the rest of the cost at a price tag that Congress keeps a secret–kind of like the gym itself.

The fact that Americans are subsidizing a gym for our public servants, when they already receive a comfy salary and can surely pay for a private gym membership on their own, is ridiculous. But what's even more frustrating is how members of Congress believe that their gym is more important than the struggles of the average American people.

For example, in 2013, the government had to shut down because Congress couldn't agree on a spending bill. The shutdown had a huge impact on Americans who were battling cancer, because the National Institutes of Health had to furlough 75 percent of their staff.[2] This resulted in the NIH having to turn away hundreds of cancer patients, including more than thirty children, from clinical trials. Many of the cancer patients who were trying to get on the clinical trials were told that they had only a couple years to live, some less, and yet they could not access potentially lifesaving treatment until government operations resumed.

The health of these cancer-stricken Americans wasn't that important to members of Congress. What Congress was more concerned about was keeping up their healthy lifestyle. As ill Americans suffered, members of Congress continued to lift weights in their exclusive gym and ride on the trolley that takes them around the Capitol building when they don't want to walk, because those services were deemed "essential" during the shutdown. Yep, then speaker John Boehner made sure to keep the congressional gym open during the government shutdown, deeming it essential to government operations. But the clinical cancer trials were not.

A Time for Four Seasons

In May 2013, while Americans lucky enough to afford a vacation were worrying about the cost of gas and metro fares for their traveling families, almost a dozen members of Congress arrived at the Four Seasons in Azerbaijan's capital of Baku. With family members, they strolled through the hotel's luxurious lobby, thanked the obsequious bellhops who carried their luggage, and settled into spacious rooms with beautiful balconies overlooking the glistening Caspian Sea. As they pondered whether to visit the city's world-famous Nizami Museum, the stunning Fire Mountain, or the region's mud volcanoes, each one of them was able to smile at the thought that this exotic respite in the oil-rich Asian autocracy wasn't costing any of them a dime.

Here's how it works. When a nonprofit special interest group has a public policy agenda that it would like Congress to work on, it puts together a lavish conference in an exotic location and invites members of Congress to the conference. Senators and representatives go to the event, listen to the group's point of view, and enjoy delicious food, business-class seats, and five-star lodging—all paid for. Many members of Congress invite their spouses on the trips. There are also trips that are paid for by foreign governments, which is completely legal thanks to the Mutual Educational and Cultural Exchange Act (MECEA), which was enacted in 1961. All a country has to do is ask the State Department for admittance into the program, and then members of Congress just have to report minimal information about the trip.

Congresswoman Sheila Jackson Lee was one of the members invited on the trip to the Four Seasons in Azerbaijan. Her trip cost her hosts $12,033.[3] Congressman Ruben Hinojosa took his wife, Martha. Their trip cost their hosts $19,961.[4] That same year, Representative John Garamendi and his wife took over $70,000 worth of trips.

Members of Congress argue that these trips are imperative. They say that it's necessary so that they can understand the other countries' political and cultural issues. However, many of these members are going on luxurious vacations paid for by either outside groups or foreign governments. Therefore, it's unlikely that they're actually getting an unbiased assessment of the area. Are members of Congress really going to understand a country when they're hanging out by the pool in the country's Ritz-Carlton?

Members of Congress refer to these trips as "missions," "diplomatic exchanges," and so forth. But why on earth would a special interest group or government throw out so much money to sponsor a trip for U.S. members of Congress and their spouses? It's not because these governments and groups are just really generous people. It's more likely that they see it as making an investment to buy influence from these members of Congress. Certainly, foreign travel can be essential to understanding a region and crafting policy, but this appears to be just influence peddling. Our representatives are being bought and, in exchange, get to be wined and dined in an exotic location with their family members. It's clearly a conflict of interest.

Our founding fathers recognized the possibility of a foreign government gaining influence through gifts. Louis XVI, for example, loved to give thank-you gifts to ministers and diplomats who departed France or with whom he had worked.

Alexander Hamilton, in Federalist No. 22, wrote that "one of the weak sides of republics, among their numerous advantages, is that they afford too easy an inlet to foreign corruption." He didn't know that one day foreign governments would influence members of Congress through free vacations for members and their families, but he understood the risk of foreign governments exercising undue influence through gifts and travel. This is why the founding fathers crafted an Emoluments Clause in our Constitution that prevented government officials from accepting gifts from foreign governments. Our founders wanted to prevent America from having the culture of political corruption that was rampant in Europe. It reads, "No Title of Nobility shall be granted by the United States: And no Person holding any Office of Profit or Trust under them, shall, without the Consent of the Congress, accept of any present, Emolument, Office, or Title of any kind whatever from any King, Prince, or foreign State."

This clause should be enough to prevent foreign governments from influencing our public servants, but when you have a Congress filled with unsavory characters and an American populace that is unaware of the details of many of these foreign trips, it's unlikely that the trips will be out-lawed anytime soon. Instead, Congress has tried to make it as difficult as possible for Americans to find out about their luxurious and free vacations.

In 2014 the House Committee on Ethics decided to make it impossible for Americans to find out about the free trips that members of Congress take. The committee quietly de-leted the rule requiring lawmakers to disclose their free trips to the U.S. House of Representatives' Office of the Clerk. Only after a wave of outrage from the media did the House Ethics Committee reverse its decision.

The ability of congresspeople to travel freely, with the fi-nancial help of foreign governments and special interest groups, is a reflection of how our public servants think only of themselves and act only out of self-interest. They know what they're doing is unethical—why else would they try so hard to shield their lavish lifestyle from Americans? They aren't staying at the Four Seasons for their constituents—they're staying there because they're taking advantage of ethical loopholes and the perks that come along with being a member of Congress. Thanks to their position of power, they are able to live far more lavishly than the average American. While most Americans struggle to put together enough money to take their kids on a small road trip, their represen-tatives are wining and dining in exotic locations.

Republican congressman Steve Stockman served the

Thirty-Sixth District of Texas from 2013 to 2015. As a member of Congress he took part in various foreign trips, from Costa Rica to Azerbaijan.

So what are these trips really like? Stockman assures me that they are educational and necessary. He argues that many members of Congress are ignorant about international affairs, and these trips help provide them with context: "In some of these trips, Russia, Ukraine, Middle East, China . . . there is a lack of knowledge by members of Congress—actually you'd be shocked and appalled on how little knowledge they have." He adds that when members of Congress are "making life-or-death decisions regarding other countries I think it's better to know the difference between Sunni and Shiite."

But does a public servant really need to take a luxurious trip to find out the difference between Sunni and Shiite? I'm pretty sure anyone with access to *Wikipedia* or a local library can figure that out quite easily. I make it known to Stockman that I'm not completely convinced that the trips to cozy locations (which are a good portion of the trips!) are necessary. After I give a little pushback, Stockman admits that, while all of his foreign travel was educational, not all members of Congress are going abroad for the right reasons.

Stockman then recalls a conversation he had with a member of Congress about the foreign trips he was planning. The member kept encouraging Stockman to go to Paris—he must! Stockman tells me that he couldn't figure out why this member of Congress was so focused on going to Paris. Stockman then asked the congressman, "What's there?" Stockman bursts into laughter while retelling the story. He then says that the congressman replied, "I have to go shopping!"

PACking a Punch

The typical congressperson receives more than $1 million in tax money every year to pay for staff, travel, and office supplies. But for many members of Congress, this isn't enough to ensure that they and their families are pampered in the manner to which they have become accustomed. If members of Congress find themselves without enough cash to support their lavish lifestyles, all they have to do is dip into their political action committee slush funds.

A PAC is Washington's greatest secret. A PAC raises money from wealthy individuals for the purpose of influencing political elections. There are limits to the amount of money PACs can give, though: up to $5,000 to a candidate per election cycle, and up to $15,000 to a national party per year. PACs can receive up to $5,000 from individuals. The money is purported to be used to help pay for consultants, office space, and polling, as well as donations to other candidates as a way for politicians currently in office to court favor from other officials. But many of these PACs don't actually use the funds in this manner. Instead, PACs have become a way to solicit money from supporters so that politicians can support their lavish lifestyles. PACs aren't anything new; they were created in 1935 thanks to organized labor.

The first PAC was formed by the Congress of Industrial Organizations to collect contributions from union members to give to President Franklin D. Roosevelt's reelection effort. At the time, unions weren't able to give money to candidates directly from their general treasuries, so this was a way around the laws. For much of their history, PACs were used by unions and businesses. It wasn't until recently that politicians like Democratic congressman Rob Andrews realized the personal benefits of PACs.

When Andrews decided that he wanted to attend the wedding of a donor in Scotland, he had his PAC finance it. Andrews took his wife and two daughters with him. He spent $7,725 for two rooms at the Balmoral Hotel, $16,675 on airfare, another $1,800 in flight change fees, and nearly $1,000 on meals and cab rides.[5] He even bought a $463 wedding gift from Bloomingdale's.

Then, when it came time for his daughter, Jacqueline, to graduate high school, Andrews decided to throw a bash. The invitation described the event as being "from elegant to carnival fun." But in order for Andrews to charge it to his PAC, he decided to frame the event as work related. That's why Andrews sent out a second invitation announcing that the event was a celebration of Jacqueline's graduation and also of Congressman Andrews's time in office.

And . . . voilà! It's just part of business!

But Democrats aren't the only people guilty of using PAC money for personal gain. D.C. Republicans talk a big game about being fiscally responsible, but many are anything but when it comes to their PAC money. Do you remember Republican House Majority Leader Eric Cantor–the man once rumored to become the next Speaker of the House after John Boehner? In 2014, David Brat, a relatively unknown figure, challenged Eric Cantor in the Republican primary, and Cantor was defeated. It sent shockwaves through all of Washington and especially the Republican establishment. No one could understand how incumbent Eric Cantor, who had spent more than $1 million in the lead-up to the election, lost to some random economics professor with only $122,000 and a twenty-three-year-old campaign manager. In fact, David Brat didn't even get one single PAC contribution during his entire campaign. Cantor, on the other hand, raised a total of $5 million. It was the most shocking loss in modern politics.

Cantor had a ton of money, but instead of spending the money properly, he used it to live lavishly. Cantor's story is indicative of how those in Washington think–that they are entitled to live a life of royalty. He spent a total of $168,637 at steakhouses–almost as much as David Brat spent for the entire election! Cantor spent more than $100,000 on lavish hotels, and $140,000 on private planes. He spent over $17,000 at the Beverly Hills Hotel alone. Supporters of Cantor entrusted him with their money, donating to him under the impression that he had America's best interests in mind. Instead, he used that money to live it up and thankfully was booted out in the end.

Andrews's and Cantor's use of PAC funds for personal expenses is more a rule than the exception when it comes to how members of Congress operate. There isn't a law preventing politicians from using the funds for personal expenses, so they essentially treat them as one big personal piggy bank. A significant number of these PACs fail to allocate much of their money to political candidates like they're supposed to. The bulk of the money that they raise goes to fund their expensive meals, private jets, limousines, Super Bowl tickets, stays at luxurious resorts, golf outings, babysitting, travel, and so forth. In Congressman Charlie Rangel's case, he commissioned an oil painting of himself with his PAC funds. The cost? $64,500.

Members of Congress argue that this is all just business and that they need to go to these expensive resorts, restaurants, and country clubs to meet with potential donors. They argue that it's necessary to meet them at upscale places. It's a nice excuse, but the reality is that PACs are just creating a whole new class of fat cats in Washington. The money is supposed to go to help other candidates, not to pay for our representatives' filet mignon and Nationals tickets. And there isn't anyone checking to ensure that this is a legitimate business expense and not a personal expense. Our representatives just claim the expense as somewhat related to their PACs, even though the money is usually just going to subsidize their luxurious lives.

Oh, and when members of Congress leave office, they take any leftover money with them. Yep . . . when average Americans get fired from their jobs, they probably have to cut back on expenses and maybe file for unemployment, but not our public servants. They're not commoners! Members of Congress are free to use their PAC money as they please.

So if they leave office with a good amount of money remaining in their PACs, as many members of Congress do, they can continue living the royal life that they were accustomed to while in office.

W hat's going on in Washington is an abuse of the system, and the rules are ridiculously loose. But Congress has zero interest in changing anything. Why fix something that's helping them live like the 1 percent? What incentive do they have to make a vote against their own wealth? Congress isn't going to tighten the rules, and its members clearly can't be trusted to self-police. They won't rein in their excesses unless Americans stand up and make this an important issue. Washington politicians talk a lot about the principle of fairness, but if they're really serious about inequity, how about working to close the loopholes that allow them to live such drastically different lives compared to average Americans? That would be real fairness.

It makes sense that members of Congress are so disconnected and uninterested in the American people: They are living in an entirely different world. How can they understand or even know the plight of average Americans when they live life in the lap of luxury? They continue to violate the power that we the people have entrusted in them, and they show no sign of reining in their abuses. So while average Americans struggle to pay their bills and send their kids to school, our public servants are jet-setting and golfing at the Breakers hotel in Palm Beach.

Dishonorable Pensions

Members of Congress are supposed to make $174,000 per year, but Congresswoman Joyce Beatty makes $427,323.[6] Here's how.

From 1999 to 2008, Beatty worked in the Ohio General Assembly. She then worked from 2008 to 2012 for the Ohio State University.

Of course, a pension system is designed for people who retire. But that's not the case for members of Congress like Beatty. When you combine the pension she receives for her work in Ohio, $253,323, with the salary she receives for her work in Washington, $174,000, she's bringing in $427,323 per year—every dollar of it paid for by taxpayers.

Beatty is far from the only member of Congress double-dipping from state and federal treasuries. One in five members of Congress receives two salaries from taxpayers.[7] For example, Democratic congressman James Clyburn of South Carolina accepted a $54,834 retirement pension in 2014. He has collected over $1 million in pension payments since he became a member of Congress. In 2014, Congressman Ted Poe of Texas collected $126,743 in pension payments. Congressman Joe Pitts of Pennsylvania collects $90,867 each year from the Pennsylvania State Employees' Retirement System. In 2012, members of Congress received more than $3 million from taxpayers in the form of retirement payments—all on top of the generous salaries we pay them.[8]

Meanwhile, many Americans feel stretched too thin to save money for retirement. With low salaries and the high cost of living, it just isn't an option. According to a 2013 report, more than a quarter of people ages fifty to sixty-four haven't started saving for retirement.[9] Americans are barely getting by with the money they have; they don't have extra cash to save for retirement. And unlike their representatives, they haven't figured out a way to rig the system so that they can make great salaries while also receiving lucrative pensions.

What happened to having a moral compass and being a leader? Look at Congresswoman Nita Lowey. The New York Democrat collects an annual $10,302 pension for her time in the state government, on top of her $174,000 congressional salary.[10] And did I mention that Lowey is worth a whopping $43 million?[11] It is legal for her to do this, but it seems unjust. What Lowey and other politicians are doing is unfair to hardworking taxpayers, many of whom don't have the money to save for their own retirement. So why should they have to pay two salaries for Lowey? As public servants, Lowey and others should be thinking about their constituents before themselves and should strive toward a financially manageable government.

A pension is supposed to help people through their retirement and provide them with security. But for many members of Congress, it's just some play money atop their taxpayer-funded salaries. This isn't money that's printed out of thin air; it's money coming from Americans' paychecks.

Who Moved My Sushi?

The perks also apply to federal government workers. They're able to enjoy vacations that are essentially spring breaks on taxpayers' dime. These spring breaks are disguised as "conferences" or "team-building trips." But the truth is that they're lavish and unnecessary.

In 2010 the General Services Administration stuck taxpayers with an $823,000 bill for a five-day trip to Las Vegas.[12] The trip entailed sending more than three hundred government workers to a casino resort in Vegas. The conference had a networking reception that included more than one thousand sushi rolls, costing taxpayers $7 apiece. The GSA spent over $140,000 on drinks and food alone.

Of course, what good is a feast worthy of a king if there isn't also a little entertainment from a court jester? The GSA's conference paid for a mind reader and a clown. There were also private after-parties held in the government workers' hotel rooms. All charged to taxpayers.

Even the process of picking where to have the conference was ludicrously expensive. The GSA spent more than $130,000 traveling to scout out potential locations. And when the conference was over, government workers left with a souvenir that symbolized all the frivolity and waste of their Vegas vacation. They returned home with velvet boxes filled with commemorative coins—which cost the government $6,000.

Everyone's favorite government agency, the Internal Revenue Service, is known for being equally reckless with our tax dollars. From 2010 to 2012, the IRS spent more than $49 million on conferences for its employees.[13]

In 2010 it held a conference in California that cost American taxpayers more than $4 million. And the waste started in the early stages of planning the conference. Instead of having an employee organize the event, the IRS hired event planners, which cost American taxpayers $133,000.

When the IRS employees arrived at the conference, they were greeted with cocktails and given swag bags that included plastic squirting fish, miniature stuffed animals, *Star Trek*-themed leather folders, plastic coins, and key chains. These bags cost taxpayers $64,000. Many of the IRS employees checked into their two-bedroom presidential suites at the hotel before heading to the training sessions. Although the point of the conference was supposed to be training, the IRS isn't even sure if all of the employees showed up to the educational sessions. Turns out that the agency didn't track whether their employees actually attended the workshops; they apparently didn't have to sign in.

However, if the IRS employees did attend the sessions, they had an interesting number of them to choose from. They could have attended the *Star Trek* parody training session. There was also a speaker at one of the training sessions who painted pictures of Michael Jordan, Bono, and other random people. The point of the session was to show how to be creative . . . or something. The painter cost taxpayers $17,000 in a speaking fee.[14] The IRS also wasted $11,400 on a speaker whose expertise is happiness. It's a shame the American people can't file a deduction on their next tax returns under the category of "theft" for this nonsense.

The IRS was able to pay for this stupidity from the unused funds it had left over from the money set aside for new hires. Interestingly, this was also the same year that Internal Revenue Service employees targeted conservative groups. Their argument? They didn't have enough staff and were overwhelmed with the number of applications from nonprofit groups seeking tax-exempt status. If they were overwhelmed with the amount of work, why not use the extra funds to hire more people rather than waste it on an IRS spring break in Vegas?

According to the expense records that were kept for the 2010 IRS conference, it cost taxpayers $4.1 million. But it may have cost taxpayers even more than that because the IRS didn't properly document all of the expenses. A report from the Treasury Inspector General for Tax Administration read: "While IRS management provided documentation showing the total final costs at $4.1 million, we could not obtain reasonable assurance that this amount represents a full and accurate accounting of the conference costs." According to the report, "Procedures at the time of the conference did not require IRS management to track and report actual conference costs. . . . As a result, TIGTA could not validate the conference cost reported by the IRS." So we will likely never know exactly how much of our money was wasted. The IRS would certainly never put up with American citizens screwing up their tax documents. But when you're a government agency, where wasting taxpayer dollars is the norm, you can get away with it.

In this tough economy, when Americans are feeling financially strained, you would think that the IRS would come up with a more economical way to get together and have training sessions. Nixing workshops that look like they came straight from a *Saturday Night Live* skit would be a good start. And what about Web-based video conferencing? The lack of concern for the American people isn't a Democratic thing or a Republican thing—it's a Washington thing. The bureaucrats have completely lost their moral compasses and abandoned their duty to serve the American people rather than themselves.

Come Fly with Me

Have you ever been running late to the airport, only to find yourself stuck in traffic and stressing about possibly missing your flight? And then, once you finally arrive, you can't find a parking spot, so you circle the underground garage—wasting more precious time. Finally, you find a spot, park, run to the airline desk, and are slapped with baggage fees. You begrudgingly pay the fees and run as fast as you can to your gate, only to have the desk manager say, "Sorry, we've already closed the gate."

More than likely, you've experienced at least one part of this story. This is the kind of stuff that happens to average Americans (including me . . . numerous times). However, if you happen to be one of the lucky few in Congress, you don't have to deal with any of it. When members of Congress fly, they don't fly coach or first-class; they fly congressional class.

One scheduler for a member of Congress tells me that when members leave town, booking their flights is easy. Browsing Orbitz for the best deal isn't necessary. Instead, congressional staffers pick up the phone and call a line designated by the airlines exclusively for Congress.

Once the scheduler is on the special phone line, he books multiple flights for his boss, because members of Congress don't have to pay a change fee. If for any reason they're running late and miss their flight, they can just grab the next one.

Unlike ordinary folks, members of Congress don't even have to worry about circling the parking lot. Members have prime spots reserved just for them at the Washington, D.C., airports–just steps away from the terminal. And can you guess the cost of those spots in a garage that charges you and me $22 a day? As usual, it's free.

Hillary

Standing before an audience of young students at Brown University, Hillary Clinton criticized the Bush administration and Congress for their contributions to the fiscal crisis and for raising the debt limit: "That is a massive transfer of responsibility onto each of you who is a student here tonight," she told them. "It is also a continuing deterioration in our own ability to control our fiscal destiny."

When her speech wrapped up and it was time to return

home, Clinton hopped back onto the plane that had transported her to Rhode Island. It was a private plane owned by Avenue Capital Group, a firm run by Clinton donor Marc Lasry. Lasry is also a former employer of Hillary's daughter, Chelsea.

Although Hillary took the plane to speak to the young liberal crowd about Congress's fiscal irresponsibility and the need to control our debt, she was doing exactly what she was railing against. Hillary had charged the American taxpayer for the charter flight she took to Rhode Island. In fact, she took more than two hundred private flights during her time in the Senate, costing taxpayers $225,756. But Hillary didn't just fly alone. She made sure to bring along her adviser Huma Abedin and spokesman Philippe Reines—bringing the total cost to over $500,000.

The life of a top public servant means never having to fly commercial. When Clinton was senator, she used private jets and oftentimes used the planes of corporations and political donors to get around. During Hillary's time as a senator she used the planes of Citigroup, the Coca-Cola Co., InfoUSA, Saban Capital Group, Abbott Laboratories, and more.[15] Senators pay these donors for flights with taxpayer dollars. They just dip into their taxpayer-funded accounts and pay the proportional cost of the flight. Members of the House of Representatives are given allowances to pay for travel, mail, and office expenses that range from $1,195,554 to $1,370,009.[16] Senators, on the other hand, are given allowances between $2,984,433 and $4,722,299.[17] In 2013, our public servants in the Senate spent $1 million on private planes.[18]

Two of the biggest spenders on private planes are Democratic senators Kirsten Gillibrand and Charles Schumer of New York. They both regularly charter flights from Washington, D.C., to areas in New York that have affordable commercial flight and train options. They both can take the train to New York, but when you've got a comfy congressional allowance, why not just take a chartered flight? An aide to Schumer argues that his tough schedule is what forces him to use taxpayer dollars for private flights.

That's the difference: When our public servants have difficult schedules, all they have to do is dip into the taxpayer piggy bank. Thanks to the American taxpayer, they are able to avoid the creepy Transportation Security Administration officer patting them down, yet they force that upon us.

A private plane should be the absolute last resort and should be used only if it's an emergency. If members of Congress are unable to make a commercial flight, then they ought to rearrange their schedule. Unfortunately, our members use chartered planes as if it's akin to calling a cab or an Uber driver.

The gap between the way of life of the governed and the governing in America is like night and day. Washington politicians are living such drastically different lives compared to the average American that they can't comprehend the concerns and the anxieties of the American people. This is creating a crisis of governance. How can our representatives understand our needs when they are both figuratively and literally out of touch with us? They've become a royal class who can't stomach the idea of having to sit in coach, or even first-class, next to regular American citizens. They refuse to mingle with the common people, but have the audacity to then bill us for their isolated lifestyles.

They purport to understand the needs of the average family, but aside from visiting their constituents when election season rolls around, they have very little connection with the ordinary lives of Americas.

Comcast

When Ryan Block needed to cancel his service with Comcast, the experience was so maddening that he decided to record it. The call was so surreal that he even asked the agent if the call was some sort of prank. He just wanted to cancel the service, but the Comcast agent on the line was determined not to let it happen. Each time Block asked for his service to be canceled the agent would just aggressively question him:

"You don't want something that works?"

"Why is it that you don't want the service?"

"So you're not interested in the fastest Internet in the country?"

"Why is that?"

"Help me understand why you don't want fast speed?"

"I'm really ashamed to see you go to something that can't give you what we can!"

"Why not keep what you know works?"

"So you don't want something that works?"

Ryan Block uploaded the audio of the conversation on his SoundCloud account, and it instantly went viral.[19] Millions of people listened and shared it because it perfectly captured how terrible it is to deal with Comcast's customer service and how frustrating it is for many Americans, myself included, whose only option for a cable provider in their area is Comcast. It reminded people of the nightmare that is Comcast: the missed appointments, the unexpected fees, the lack of customer service, and so forth. Their service reputation is so poor that it has earned them *Consumerist*'s "Worst Company in America" award twice, first in 2010 and then in 2014.[20]

If you're an average American Comcast customer, you're probably not surprised that Comcast has won this award more than once. On the other hand, if you are part of the Washington elite and are a customer of Comcast, you likely haven't had to experience the awful service at all.

According to legal documents, the Washington Comcast office–Comcast Cablevision of Potomac–keeps a list of elected and influential officials in Washington who are Comcast customers.[21] Comcast refuses to explain why they have a special list and denies that politicians receive special treatment. Yet they have a government affairs team that carries around VIP cards with special codes. The cards are given to journalists, congressional staffers, and members of the Washington elite.[22] Comcast gives them to all of the Washington power players in hopes of improving their terrible reputation and getting regulatory approval.

How does it work? According to *Consumerist,* when an elite Washingtonian calls the Comcast customer service line, the system recognizes their number and automatically directs them to the front of the call line–ahead of all the average Americans who have been waiting patiently to speak to a Comcast agent.

Some important Washingtonians have never been specifically told they are on this VIP list and get expedited service from Comcast. So when they call, they get preferential treatment and probably can't understand why so many Comcast customers hate the company so much.

Comcast's preferential treatment for the powerful in Washington doesn't just stop at VIP cards and customer service. In 2014, the Senate Judiciary Committee met to discuss the controversial $45 billion merger of Comcast and Time Warner Cable. The committee is composed of Republicans and Democrats who are usually diametrically opposed to one another, but not when it comes to the issue of Comcast cash. Every single senator, Republican or Democrat, who sat on the Senate Judiciary Committee had received money from Comcast's PAC.[23] And the House side wasn't much better. Comcast's PAC had given thirty-two of the thirty-nine members of the House Judiciary Committee checks.[24]

If you're a member of the Washington political class, expect VIP treatment and/or money from Comcast.

If you're an average American with Comcast, best of luck dealing with the most hated company in America (minus Washington, D.C.).

Air Farce One

In 2006, the satirical *Onion* ran a pretty funny story titled "Flustered Bush Misses Air Force One Flight." It reports that the president lost his car keys, got stuck in traffic, was slowed down by a long security line, raced through the terminal, and arrived at the departure gate just before Air Force One took off for Idaho. Because of strict guidelines prohibiting the airline personnel from opening the door to the plane within fifteen minutes of takeoff, Bush was shut out, even though the plane was still on the tarmac. A frustrated Bush complained, "Now my biggest suitcase is halfway to who-knows-where and I'm stuck in this stupid airport." He was offered a standby seat on a flight to Reno, but he didn't see "how that helps [him] in the slightest."

In reality, Air Force One doesn't just protect presidents from many of the inconveniences everyone else faces. It also exposes some presidents'–in particular, President Obama's–farcical hypocrisy on environmental matters.

Consider, for example, Earth Day 2014. The president heralded the day by proclaiming, "I, BARACK OBAMA, President of the United States of America, by virtue of the authority vested in me by the Constitution and the laws of the United States, do hereby proclaim April 22, 2014, as Earth Day. I encourage all Americans to participate in programs and activities that will protect our environment and contribute to a healthy, sustainable future."

But as Obama's itinerary that day demonstrated, his proclamation was meant for you–not him. He wanted you to alter your lifestyle to "protect our environment and contribute to a healthy, sustainable future," even though he had no intention of changing his lifestyle or leading by example. He was about to embark on a trip to Washington State and Japan that would burn an estimated thirty-eight thousand gallons of fuel.[25]

Just imagine it: It's ten A.M. and Marine One is waiting for the president. The president is running fifteen minutes late. Meanwhile, Marine One's engines are idling, releasing toxins into the air.

When the president finally arrives, he heads to Joint Base Andrews to board Air Force One. He boards his plane and heads to Paine Field in Washington State.

While the president is en route in his environmentally unfriendly plane, dozens of people in Washington State are preparing for the president's arrival. Fire trucks, black SUVs, motorcycle troopers, and police cars are parked beside the airfield where the president is set to arrive. The cars, trucks, and SUVS are idling and emitting pollution into the air.

Meanwhile, Secret Service agents shine their cars with a dust rag and make sure the small American flags perched upon them are upright and straight. Neither the king-like pomp nor the hypocritical carbon emissions are of any concern to the president on this Earth Day.

These stories would disappoint our founding fathers, but they wouldn't surprise Thomas Jefferson. He warned of the dangers of an active government, consolidating power in D.C., and having a large executive branch. He admitted to Hamilton that he was "not a friend to a very energetic government. . . . It is always oppressive." The thinking was that the less money and power the federal government had, the less opportunity there would be for corruption, self-serving perks, and abuse. He mistrusted the executive branch because he thought it too closely resembled a monarchy and believed that big government risked creating a royal class that would waste "the labors of the people under the pretense of taking care of them." He often referred to those who advocated for a strong executive branch as "monocrats."

It's clear that Jefferson's warnings were warranted and that the monocrats are winning. The reason why Washington officials are able to get away with spending our money on over-the-top cars, spring break conferences, and taxpayer-funded private jets is because of what Jefferson warned us of—the steady escalation of their power. Power brings more opportunity for waste and more ego. The Washington elite don't see anything wrong with what they are doing because they feel as though they are entitled to these things. The taxpayer may not think that they deserve those perks, but when you live and work in a town filled with people who view themselves as royals—and better than average Americans—this is the result.

Jefferson was equally concerned when he would see government getting involved with private business. He feared that the country would end up with a "single and splendid government of an aristocracy, founded on banking institutions, and moneyed incorporations under the guise and cloak of their favored branches of manufactures, commerce and navigation, riding and ruling over the plundered ploughman and beggared yeomanry." He added that it would be a "surest stepping-stone to" a monarchy.

There are no better examples of this than the cases of Comcast and the airlines. Private business and government are intertwined now. Comcast executives want to provide financial support and preferential service to government employees because they know that their future decisions will affect their business's profits and livelihood. Similarly, the airlines want to be as accommodating as possible to politicians because it's the politicians in D.C. who decide whether or not the airlines will be further regulated. The more interconnected private business and government become, the cozier they'll get and the more perks politicians will receive.

Thomas Jefferson would be troubled if he could see how expansive and monarchical the presidency has become. But for those in Washington today who get to enjoy the monarchical life that Jefferson warned of, it's just another day of Versailles on the Potomac.

CHAPTER 3

Do as We Say, Not as We Do

I n 325 B.C., Alexander the Great led his army on a sixty-day march through the scorching Gedrosian desert. There was not nearly enough water for his men, and soldiers everywhere were collapsing from dehydration. One day, scouts returned to camp after finding enough water to fill an entire helmet. They offered the helmet of precious water to the thirsty and dry-throated Alexander, but he took the helmet, held it high for all to see, and poured it into the desert sand. If his soldiers could not drink, Alexander would not drink, either.

Alexander the Great was able to conquer the known world because the men he led respected him. They believed in themselves because their commander believed in them. They knew he would never ask them to do anything he wouldn't expect of himself. He would fight with them, suffer with them, and even thirst with them. He was no hypocrite. That's what leadership is all about (although Alexander's men undoubt-edly would have preferred for him to share the water rather than waste it on a dramatic gesture).

Unfortunately, our nation is governed today by one of the most hypocritical institutions in American history—the federal government. While the ruling elite frequently make laws requiring average Americans to endure hardships and change their lifestyles, people in power exempt themselves from the sacrifices they expect ordinary people to make. The rules they make—from Obamacare to the Americans with Disabilities Act, the Freedom of Information Act, and even the prohibition against insider trading—apply to us, not to them.

If You (I) Like Your (My) Plan, You (I) Can Keep It

In 2013, millions of Americans received letters notifying them that they would have to sign up for healthcare on the Obamacare exchanges. This was shocking to most Americans. On some thirty-six occasions, President Obama said a variation of "If you like your healthcare plan, you can keep it." At one point he said, "If you like your current insurance, you keep that insurance. Period. End of story."

Unfortunately, the president lied. Many Americans learned in the fall of 2013 that not only would they be un-able to keep their health insurance plans, but they would also have to pay higher premiums for their new plans.

One of those deceived Americans was Edie Littlefield

Sundby of California. Edie fought gallbladder cancer for seven years. In 2013, writing in the *Wall Street Journal,* she explained that because of Obamacare, she would no longer be able to have the affordable medical insurance policy that helped save her life. Obamacare forced her out of the network of doctors she trusted—doctors who had saved her life by battling stage-four cancer.

Edie's story isn't unique. Her unfortunate situation happened to many other Americans. President Obama made a promise to America at a time when he needed every possible ounce of support to get Obamacare through Congress, and after his bill became the law, he blithely admitted that his promise had been false.

Adding insult to injury, the people responsible for Obamacare created exemptions to the law for themselves. Here's what happened.

When Obamacare was still in its infancy, Senator Chuck Grassley introduced an amendment that made sure all staff members would have to sign up for Obamacare. The thinking was that if Congress had a personal stake in the law, they would make sure that the law improved healthcare. If it didn't, the law would harm its creators just as much as it harmed their constituents.

But once staffers on Capitol Hill saw that Obamacare would raise their premiums and force them to change their doctors, they wanted to keep their old plan through the Federal Employees Health Benefits Program. Of course, one solution would have been to repeal Obamacare. But that would have meant admitting that they had been wrong to support it. So instead they did what political insiders do best–they created a loophole.

The Office of Personnel Management created a special rule for Capitol Hill. The rule said that if congressional staffers were deemed "unofficial," they could keep their old health plans. Of course, OPM made sure to allow each individual congressional office to determine who is "official" and who is "unofficial." When I called the Senate disbursing office and House payroll and benefits office, they, unsurprisingly, made it clear that they were unwilling to give out the number of staffers in Congress who were deemed "official or unofficial." And just to sweeten the deal, OPM decided that congressional staffers buying healthcare on an Obamacare exchange would also get a $10,000-per-family subsidy from the government–courtesy of the taxpayers who were suffering under the law these political insiders were escaping.

Believe it or not, the people responsible for Obamacare didn't stop there. While they didn't lift a hand to exempt individuals from Obamacare's onerous burdens, they gave their favorite businesses a one-year exemption from the law's devastating effects. Congresswoman Nancy Pelosi's district got 20 percent of the first round of Obamacare waivers issued in 2011. Many of the lucky recipients were upscale restaurants and hotels. For example, an upscale eatery in her district, Boboquivari's, received a waiver. An entrée at this eatery ranges from $30 to $60. The five-star luxury hotel Taj Campton Place, where the average room costs $1,000, got a waiver as well. Hotel Nikko in San Francisco, another upscale hotel, also got a waiver. Large companies and labor unions also received Obamacare waivers, including the United Federation of Teachers, which is affiliated with the American Federation of Teachers. Not surprisingly, in 2008 they threw almost $2 million behind the election of President Obama. Meanwhile, Edie Littlefield Sundby and others were being forced into overpriced insurance plans and away from the doctors who had saved their lives.

No longer do we live in system where our leaders are willing to stand up and work through the tough times with their people. Instead, they stand tall with their friends while the American people continue to suffer.

Estate Tax

"The estate tax has been historically part of our very fundamental belief that we should have a meritocracy, that we do not want a system where we expect people to make it on their own—to be, over time, dominated by inherited wealth," said Hillary Clinton at a joint event with billionaire Warren Buffett. She argued that the estate tax is needed in order to shrink the growing gap between the wealthy and the poor in America. Ideally, Clinton would like to see a higher estate tax—setting the tax rate at 45 percent—and a lower personal exemption. "It's not as though people will be destitute," Clinton argued. While in the Senate she made sure to vote against any measures that would provide relief from the estate tax to small businesses and families. For example, she voted no on the Economic Growth and Tax Relief Reconciliation Act of 2001, which would have provided estate tax exemptions. She voted no on the Death Tax Repeal Permanency Act of 2005, and the Estate Tax and Extension of Tax Relief Act of 2006.

Clinton publicly argues that the estate tax, a hefty tax against a person who inherits property, is essential for economic justice in America. When it comes to other people's wealth, the Clintons want to level the playing field, but when it comes to their own money, they will do everything possible to avoid the tax structure that they publicly support.

The Clintons have been able to amass a small fortune through their speaking engagements and book deals, and they want to make sure they keep as much of that money as possible. Behind the scenes, the Clintons have assembled a team of financial strategists who have helped protect them from the estate tax. The Clintons talk a big game about closing loopholes, but privately they're using an estate tax loophole to keep their money away from Uncle Sam.

In order to avoid the brunt of the estate tax, the Clintons divided up their New York home into two 50 percent shares and placed it into shared trusts. The tax advantage of doing so is that if the value of their home increases, it will increase outside of their taxable state. They can later claim a lesser value for their home.[1] This will help prevent hundreds of thousands of their dollars from going to the government.[2] This is a common financial strategy among the very wealthy in America, but blatantly hypocritical coming from a wealthy family that advocates for these policies.

But the hypocrisy doesn't just apply to taxation; it also applies to education policy.

In the 1980s Utah senator Orrin Hatch tried to push for school choice as a way to revive the public education system in America. The idea is to give Americans more control over education by offering parents the option to send their child to whatever school they feel best meets their needs. The government would give families a voucher that covers the cost of education for a child and will allow them to decide which school, either public or private, they want to send their child to. Proponents believe this will promote competition among schools and increase their performance.

Hatch's plan would have allowed low-income families in Washington, D.C., to send their children to the school of their choice. He began pushing for school choice under Reagan, but the idea was ultimately killed when President Bill Clinton vetoed it. He deprived thousands of kids the opportunity to go to the school of their choice.

Hillary Clinton is also against the idea of school vouchers. When she was a senator she argued in a speech that giving Americans the option to choose their school would inevitably lead to children attending "the school of the White Supremacist." The former senator continued: "So what if the next parent comes and says, 'I want to send my child to the School of Jihad'? I won't stand for it."

She obviously ignored the fact that a voucher program would require children in America to attend schools that have been accredited by the state, thus not allowing them to go to a school of extremism. But it doesn't really matter, because this issue affects your kid–not hers.

When it comes to a poor American family, the children have no choice but to attend the public school in their neighborhood. As president, Bill Clinton deprived parents of the opportunity to put their children in the best school. However, when it came to his daughter, he made sure she had the best education.

When Hillary and Bill arrived in Washington, D.C., they didn't put Chelsea into the school in their district. Instead, they put their daughter into an elite pre-kindergarten through twelfth-grade private school, Sidwell Friends School, in northwest Washington. The cost of an education at Sidwell Friends? $37,750 a year, not including additional fees.

Now, you can't fault the Clintons for sending their child to the best and most elite school–everyone wants what's best for their children. That's fine. However, they shouldn't deny other Americans that same opportunity. Shouldn't people who live in Washington, D.C., have the option to send their child to the school of their choosing, rather than the school chosen for them by the government?

Nationally, as of 2015, only 10 percent of Americans send their kids to private school.[3] But if you look at Congress, the picture looks a bit different. According to the Heritage Foundation, as of 2009, 44 percent of senators and 36 percent of House members had at one time sent their children to private schools.[4] They want to be able to do what's best for their family, but they want to deprive average Americans of that opportunity.

Hypocrite22@clintonemail.com

In 2012, Hillary attended the first meeting of the Open Government Partnership, an initiative whose goal is to promote transparency, empower taxpayers, and battle corruption in government. More than a thousand representatives from various countries attended the meeting.

At the event, Hillary declared that "the cure for corruption is openness." She added that "by belonging to the Open Government Partnership, every country here is sending a message to their own people that we will stand for openness."

Later in the speech Clinton added, "I've seen how technology is transforming the way that we and other nations do diplomacy and development . . . but, of course, technology isn't some kind of magic wand. Ultimately, it is political will that determines whether or not we hold ourselves accountable."

Publicly, Hillary positioned herself as a champion for openness and pressured other countries to be more transparent with their citizens. And because of her efforts as secretary of state to bring awareness to the ideas of government transparency, she was awarded the 2012 Transparency International-USA's Integrity Award. While she publicly purported to be a champion of transparency, secretly she was doing everything in her power to circumvent rules and shield her electronic communications.

On March 14, 2013, a hacker who went by the name of Guccifer broke into the AOL account of Sidney Blumenthal, a former White House aide to Bill Clinton and a friend of Hillary Clinton. The hacker, a Romanian man whose real name was Marcel-Lehel Lazar, sent screen shots of Hillary's in-box to journalists. The emails included information about the attacks in Benghazi, Libya, and advice from Blumenthal to Hillary.

What stood out from the emails was the fact that Blumenthal's correspondence with Hillary Clinton, then secretary of state, was not sent to her government email account. The information they discussed–Benghazi and Libya–would clearly fall under official State Department business, so why wasn't she using the department's email address?

Turns out that Hillary used mostly a personal email–hdr22@clintonemail.com–for her business correspondence.

Federal regulations require the secretary of state to send all business-related emails through her government email in order to preserve her correspondence for public record. Hillary, though, circumvented federal record-keeping rules and used her own private email account to conduct business while secretary of state.

She also took steps to create a private email server that operated out of her home in New York, so her personal email wouldn't go through typical channels that average people use, such as Yahoo or Gmail. All of her correspondence was housed on that server, which is inaccessible to State Department officials.

Why did she do this? To keep information away from taxpayers and to give her more control over what information she would reveal to them. And she succeeded.

In March 2010, the Associated Press made FOIA requests associated with Hillary's time at the State Department and her appointment of Huma Abedin to deputy chief of staff.[5] All of the requests were left unanswered. Similarly, the super PAC America Rising has submitted FOIA requests for records from the State Department over a dozen times.[6] It has yet to receive documents. Then in 2012, congressional investigators began investigating the attack in Benghazi that led to the death of J. Christopher Stevens, the U.S. ambassador to Libya. They requested documents from the State Department to try to determine what Secretary of State Clinton knew at the time and what exactly had gone wrong. They couldn't get much clarity on the situation because the State Department could hand over documents only from her public email account. Clinton's use of a private email account shielded her from congressional requests like this.

It's hard not to assume that this is exactly why Hillary had chosen to use a personal account.

To make matters even more suspicious, Hillary deleted emails stored on her private server that she sent and received during her time as secretary of state. She claims she "didn't see any reason to keep them." The server should have been given to an independent arbiter to differentiate which emails were public and which were private. However, Clinton didn't offer the public that opportunity. Instead, the decision as to what the public should be able to see was made entirely by her.

When she was forced to comply with the law and turn over emails, she was able to take all the time she wanted and could selectively choose which pieces of correspondence to hand over and make public. She deleted more than thirty thousand of her sixty thousand emails from her four-year tenure as secretary of state, arguing that they were personal and not business related. If the emails were simply just about frivolous matters, like she suggested, such as "yoga routines" and planning her daughter's wedding—why not hand those over to the State Department or an independent arbiter and allow them to determine which ones are business related?

Although President Obama promised to usher in a new era of transparency when he took office, he clearly didn't have a problem with Hillary's arrangement. According to White House Press Secretary Josh Earnest, President Obama knew that Hillary was using a private email account to conduct business. "Yes, he [Obama] was aware of her email address," he said. "He traded emails with her."

So while Clinton talks up a big game about transparency and accountability, privately she is undermining those principles.

Hillary's decision to use a private server shows that she's willing to put the American people at risk in order to maintain her reputation. Clinton claims that she never sent classified information over her private server. However, it's difficult to imagine that she never transmitted secret information via her server, considering she used her private email almost exclusively for four years. No one, not even the State Department, will ever know if she is being forthcoming. However, whether or not she sent classified information, the use of a private home server to transmit communications by a top diplomat is reckless. She created a security threat by potentially exposing the confidential business of the U.S. secretary of state to hackers.

Clinton's decision to use her own server shows that she sees herself as above the law and believes that federal disclosure laws shouldn't apply to her. Like many politicians in Washington, she wants to shield the decision-making process from the average American so that she can't be held accountable.

Hillary's lack of transparency and accountability undermines the principles of this country and creates a shadow government, where decisions are made outside the eyes of the public. The American people delegate power to those in Washington to represent us. We entrust them with this power and expect information in return to ensure that they are working on behalf of their constituents and not on behalf of themselves. Hillary has deprived people of that power and has abused her position. How can the American people hold their officials accountable, when the officials are deliberately concealing information about their work? Hillary hopes that the American people vote for her in 2016, but the American people don't have the ability to verify whether the power we gave her during her tenure as secretary of state wasn't abused. What she has turned over for the public domain may not be the entire record, but rather the record she wants us to see.

Those in Washington, whether appointed or elected, are expected to be responsive to us—the American people. Their actions and communications should be available for average Americans and journalists to scrutinize. We should have that information so that we can become better aware of the workings of Washington and make more informed decisions when it's time for us to cast our ballots. It's also imperative to the health and stability of our democracy that journalists in America get information like this. How can the American press be a proper watchdog when our politicians are infringing on reporters' right to search for public information that's in the interest of the American people? We have a right to access information about Clinton's time as secretary of state, yet she has denied the American people that opportunity. While she makes grand speeches about the need for other countries to become transparent, she is working to conceal her work from her own country.

Too Ugly for Me

In 2001, Jim Gordon, a private developer from Energy Management, proposed the idea of putting together the United States' first-ever offshore wind farm. It would provide power for hundreds of thousands of households without pollution emissions on Cape Cod, Nantucket, and Martha's Vineyard. The idea won the support and praise of almost all environmental groups. They viewed it as the beginning of a "green" revolution in America and the start of a trend toward sustainable energy. However, green energy champions like Democratic senator Ted Kennedy of Massachusetts and his nephew Robert F. Kennedy Jr. ended up becoming Jim Gordon's fiercest critics.

One would think that Ted Kennedy, who was a supporter

of clean energy, would have liked the idea of bringing clean energy to Hyannis Port. Similarly, one would expect his nephew Robert F. Kennedy Jr., a prominent environmental attorney and activist, to support the plan. But the two Kennedys did no such thing.

Why not? Because the Kennedy family would have a view of the wind farm from their pristine private beach.

The 130 wind turbines would be five miles off the coast of the beach, and the Kennedys' concern was that it would ruin the aesthetics of their neighborhood and damage the value of their homes.

Writing in the *New York Times,* Robert F. Kennedy Jr. said:

> As an environmentalist, I support wind power, including wind power on the high seas. I am also involved in siting wind farms in appropriate landscapes, of which there are many. But I do believe that some places should be off limits to any sort of industrial development. I wouldn't build a wind farm in Yosemite National Park. Nor would I build one on Nantucket Sound, which is exactly what the company Energy Management is trying to do with its Cape Wind project. Cape Wind's proposal involves construction of 130 giant turbines whose windmill arms will reach 417 feet above the water and be visible for up to 26 miles. These turbines are less than six miles from shore and would be seen from Cape Cod, Martha's Vineyard and Nantucket. Hundreds of flashing lights to warn airplanes away from the turbines will steal the stars and nighttime views.[7]

Translation: I'm an environmentalist when it's convenient for me. I believe that some places should be off limits, like, my places. I wouldn't build this project in Yosemite National Park or anywhere close to my home, but your neighborhood sounds good. Yep. I'm okay with green energy stealing the stars and nighttime views above your home, but don't steal mine.

Are you unconvinced that his neighborhood is akin to a great national park? He continues:

> There are those who argue that unlike our great Western national parks, Cape Cod is far from pristine, and that Cape Wind's turbines won't be a significant blot. I invite these critics to see the pods of humpback, minke, pilot, finback, and right whales off Nantucket, to marvel at the thousands of harbor and gray seals lolling on the bars off Monomoy and Horseshoe Shoal, to chase the dark clouds of terns and shorebirds descending over the thick menhaden schools exploding over acre-sized feeding frenzies of striped bass, bluefish and bonita.

Translation: My neighborhood is gorgeous and, let's be honest, yours isn't as beautiful. So I'm for green energy in *your* backyard.

The then senator John Kerry shared some of the same feelings as Robert F. Kennedy. Responding to a question on his website about the proposal, Kerry said, "You can't just have someone plunk something down wherever the hell they want." He then questioned "whether this is the best location."

Again, it's okay in your backyard, just not okay in the backyard of the politically elite and well connected.

This is a project that green energy advocates like Robert F. Kennedy Jr. should support. If one truly believes that the ocean is warming, that humans are destroying the planet, and that climate change is today's greatest threat (as he does), then he should view these turbines as a step in the right direction. When he stares out of his beautiful, lavish compound and sees the turbines, he shouldn't view them as ugly. Rather, one would expect that an environmentalist would view them as a reminder that green energy is (apparently) going to save the planet for our children, grandchildren, and future generations. Furthermore, if you own a compound on the beach and believe that our beaches are threatened, then you should presumably want this the most. Right?

But that's not how the political elite work. They like to attend their environmental protests (via private SUV and airplane) and tell everyone else to give up their SUVs. They like to lecture America about how we need clean energy. Meanwhile, they can't even stomach the idea of having a less than perfect ocean view from their compound for the sake of their cause.

After a nine-year federal review process, the project got approval from the Obama administration. Robert F. Kennedy Jr. was devastated, declaring that "[Ted Kennedy] would be heartbroken."[8]

Ah, yes, Ted Kennedy, champion of green energy, must

be rolling in his grave at the thought of his picturesque views from his family's compound being marred by wind turbines—you know, those things he advocated for. Poor guy.

Not in My Backyard

"We are not a country that should turn children away and send them back to certain death," said then Maryland governor Martin O'Malley at a National Governors Association meeting in Nashville. He was speaking about the recent surge of unaccompanied illegal immigrant children crossing the border into the United States. At the time, there were as many as eighty thousand children who had crossed the border illegally and were being held in Texas.

He urged the country and the Obama administration to show compassion toward the children and criticized the care they were receiving when they were admitted into U.S. custody. He referred to the facilities that were housing the illegal immigrant children as "kennels."

The speech won him praise from the left for showing compassion over what many reporters and politicians referred to as a humanitarian crisis. He urged the American people to allow these children who crossed into the United States illegally to stay rather than deport them back to their country. But what O'Malley didn't express to the room of reporters was that he is in favor of keeping illegal immigrant children in the United States, so long as they aren't in his backyard.

After O'Malley made his bleeding-heart-liberal speech to the crowd of reporters, he called up the White House to express a quite different point of view.

O'Malley spoke to a top White House official, Cecilia Muñoz, about the Department of Health and Human Services' proposal to send these young children to Maryland. The government didn't want to deport them, so there was an urgent need to house thousands of children.

The White House and HHS needed temporary facilities immediately and were interested in a short-term lease at a facility in Maryland so that they could house, feed, and provide care for hundreds of illegal children who had come unaccompanied to the United States.

O'Malley's answer: Hell no.

The same man who had lectured Americans wanting to deport illegal immigrants, saying, "Through all of our great world religions, we are told that hospitality to strangers is an essential human dignity," was now unwilling to accommodate these strangers. O'Malley expressed to the White House that he felt his constituents wouldn't be receptive to these new young strangers and so he didn't want them in the facility.[9]

But O'Malley isn't the only one who purports to care about the needs of illegal immigrants publicly, while privately doing the opposite. Democratic governor Dan Malloy of Connecticut had a firm message for the federal government when it came knocking on his door asking for a facility to house the illegal children: Not in my state!

Malloy's reputation as pro–illegal immigrants has won

him praise from the left. In fact, because of his stance on immigration issues, the *Daily Beast* has called Malloy the "progressives' dream governor."[10] Malloy seemed like the perfect politician for federal officials to work with on the housing crisis for illegal immigrants. So federal officials had their eyes on a facility in Connecticut, specifically the Southbury Training School, as a potential place to house two thousand young illegals in the United States.

Federal officials were surprised when they received an email from Connecticut's Office of Policy and Management with a detailed list of the reasons why it wouldn't be a good idea to bring the children to Connecticut. The main argument was that the building wasn't in great shape.

Patrick M. O'Brien, assistant director of OPM's Bureau of Assets Management, wrote to an official at the U.S. General Services Administration's New England regional offices:

> Southbury Training School is home to adults in State care with developmental disabilities." Their families and the developmentally disabled community keep a watchful eye on the residents and the property itself. Any new and significant activity at Southbury would be intensively scrutinized by a multitude of interest groups and organizations, and would face time-consuming challenges.[11]

O'Brien added: "The State of Connecticut simply does not own appropriate facilities that can accommodate these needs."

Your backyard. Not mine.

ADA? What ADA?

There are many other laws that you, the average American, must follow, but that Congress doesn't. One of them is the Americans with Disabilities Act.

The ADA was passed by Congress in 1990. It prohibits discrimination based on disability and applies to employers with fifteen or more employees. Although the policy is great in theory, it has unfortunately led to endless litigation for American business owners, especially when they are targeted by serial ADA scammers.

One of those ADA scammers is Alfredo Garcia. A convicted felon and an illegal immigrant whose case is still making its way through immigration courts, Garcia became disabled after falling out of a tree while he was intoxicated and high on cocaine. This ne'er-do-well hasn't held a job since, but he has supported himself by suing small businesses. Since his injury, he has earned over $1 million from business owners.

Garcia's weapon has been the Americans with Disabilities Act. He's filed more than eight hundred lawsuits against businesses in California—many of them just ma-and-pa shops—for alleged violations of the ADA.[12] Suits by people like Garcia claim that a bathroom mirror isn't low enough, or that there aren't enough signs directing people to a restroom.

In effect, these serial litigants are exploiting technicalities in the ADA to extort American business owners, for whom the ADA has been a disaster. But meanwhile, the government big shots in Washington don't have to worry about

the ADA, because they've exempted themselves from its requirements.

If you're ever in Washington, D.C., just take a stroll
around Capitol Hill, and you can see the evidence for yourself. The sidewalks around the offices for the House don't
comply with the ADA. The bathrooms in the building don't
comply with ADA. Neither do the Senate's, or those in the
Library of Congress. The curbs around the Capitol don't
comply either. A whopping 93 percent of them violate the
ADA.[13] It's another example of a law in which members of
Congress make sure that they don't have to pay the costs they
impose on the people they are supposed to represent.

But Congress enacted the Americans with Disabilities
Act! They patted themselves on the back and convinced
themselves, and the rest of America, that they had made history by forcing businesses to provide accommodations for
the disabled. But if they cared so much about the disabled,
why haven't they done anything to accommodate the disabled in their workplace? Well, it's because helping the disabled wasn't ever their priority. Instead, it was about helping
out big business.

I spoke to Doug Wead, former special assistant to President George H. W. Bush, about the Americans with Disabilities Act. I initially asked him whether he witnessed corruption
during his time working in Washington, D.C., and he turned
the conversation to the ADA, which was enacted in 1990
under his boss. "I saw the beginnings of corruption," he told
me. "Regulation is a good example [of corruption]. . . . As
you know, companies create regulations to create monopo-

lies. . . . The old barons, they would drive the price down to get you out of business and then they'd raise the price." He argued that regulatory legislation like the ADA is the way big businesses try to push out competition: "The new barons, they regulate you out of existence so that you can't start." They do this by preventing small businesses from ever entering the market. "If you're an African American couple and you graduate from college and you want to start a hamburger joint," Wead said, "you've got so many regulations that are in place that all of the big companies—the restaurant chains—have favored and promoted and won kudos" for from the government. As a new business it's difficult to comply with all of the regulations under the ADA and, if you don't comply and happen to be sued, ADA litigation can force you out of business. It's awful for small businesses, but great for big business.

And that is what the Americans with Disabilities Act is all about. Congress enacted it not to help people with disabilities, but to help the big businesses they had relationships with.

"The Americans with Disabilities Act—that's what was happening when I was in the White House," says Wead about the corruption he witnessed in D.C. "They wanted that [the ADA] not because they cared about disabled people but because they sought a device to drive their competitors out of the marketplace." They understood that big businesses wanted this in order to prevent new, smaller, family-owned businesses from entering into the marketplace, and they helped them.

So it makes sense that Congress doesn't comply with the legislation that they passed. They didn't enact these laws because they truly care about people with disabilities. They did it because they saw it as an opportunity to grant a favor to big business (you scratch my back, I'll scratch yours). It also confirms their sense of superiority and feeds their ego. They can grandstand about how they worked to help out the disadvantaged . . . even if that was the last thing they were trying to do.

What Is Congress Hiding?

Earl Glynn is a blogger from Kansas. When Congress was debating the controversial American Clean Energy and Security Act of 2009–the cap and trade bill–Glynn decided he wanted to figure out how many calls, for and against the legislation, his member of Congress was getting from constituents.

Glynn had heard of the Freedom of Information Act–a law requiring government officials to disclose documents requested by concerned citizens. The government's FOIA website describes the law as one "that keeps citizens in the know about their government." So Glynn decided to make a FOIA request of his member of Congress to get this information.

Can you guess what happened? Glynn received a simple response from his member of Congress: "FOIA doesn't apply to Congress." Once again, Congress exempted its members from a law that they enacted.

To show how one-sided this exemption is, consider that

FOIA applies to the Department of Agriculture, the Department of Commerce, the Department of Defense, the Department of Education, the Department of Energy, the Department of Health and Human Services, the Department of Homeland Security, the Department of Housing and Urban Development, the Department of the Interior, the Department of Justice, the Department of Labor, the Department of State, the Department of Transportation, the Department of the Treasury, the Department of Veterans Affairs, the Internal Revenue Service, the Social Security Administration, the Immigration and Naturalization Service, the Federal Election Commission, the Federal Trade Commission, the Federal Communications Commission, the Nuclear Regulatory Commission, the U.S. Agency for International Development, the Environmental Protection Agency, the National Labor Relations Board, the Occupational Safety and Health Review Commission, and the Securities and Exchange Commission.

But not to Congress.

REPORTER: Did you consider that to be a conflict of interest?

NANCY PELOSI: I don't know what your point is of your question.

The hypocrisy of the government applies to insider trading as well. When average American citizens trade stocks with private information that affects stock prices, they end up in prison. But when you're Congresswoman Nancy Pelosi or Senator Dick Durbin, you're exempt.

In 2008, Nancy Pelosi put herself in a position to make $80,000 off insider information. In July of that year, the chairman of the House Judiciary Committee introduced the Credit Card Fair Fee Act. If the bill had become a law, it would have drastically reduced the profits of credit card companies like Visa by allowing businesses to negotiate lower credit card fees. Understandably, the credit card industry was vehemently opposed to it.

But concerns about the impact of the Credit Card Fair Fee Act on credit card companies didn't stop Speaker of the House Nancy Pelosi and her husband from investing in Visa while the fate of the Credit Card Fair Fee Act was uncertain. In 2008, after the act had been introduced, the Pelosi family participated in a Visa IPO.

As Steve Kroft of *60 Minutes* reported, "Undisturbed by a potential conflict of interest, the Pelosis purchased 5,000 shares of Visa at the initial price of $44 dollars. Two days later it was trading at $64. The credit card legislation never made it to the floor of the House."

In other words, in just a few days, the value of the Pelosi family's stock portfolio increased by $80,000, thanks to a stock that would likely have fallen if the Congress she led had not killed the Credit Card Fair Fee Act. When asked about this form of insider trading—one of at least eight times Pelosi has traded on information unavailable to the public—her defense was barely articulate:

KROFT: Madam Leader, I wanted to ask you why you
and your husband back in March of 2008 accepted

and participated in a very large IPO deal from Visa at a time there was major legislation affecting the credit card companies making its way through the–through the House.

REP. PELOSI: But–

MR. KROFT: And did you consider that to be a conflict of interest?

REP. PELOSI: The–y–I–I don't know what your point is of your question. Is there some point that you want to make with that?

MR. KROFT: Well, I–I–I guess what I'm asking is do you think it's all right for a Speaker to accept a very preferential, favorable stock deal?

REP. PELOSI: Well, we didn't.

MR. KROFT: You participated in the IPO. And at the time you were Speaker of the House. You don't think it was a conflict of interest or had the appearance–

REP. PELOSI: No, it was not–

MR. KROFT: –of a conflict of interest?

REP. PELOSI: –it doesn't–it only has appearance if you decide that you're going to have–elaborate on a false premise. But it–it–it's not true and that's that.

MR. KROFT: I don't understand what part's not true.

REP. PELOSI: Yes, sir. That–that I would act upon an investment.[14]

Unfortunately, Nancy Pelosi isn't the only one guilty of insider trading. On September 19, 2008, Senator Dick Durbin of Illinois went into a closed meeting with Treasury Secretary Hank Paulson and Chairman Ben Bernanke of the Federal Reserve about the financial crisis.[15] During this time, Paulson was trying to scare members of Congress about the economy so that they would pass his Troubled Asset Relief Program plan.

The very next day, Durbin sold over $40,000 in mutual fund shares.

After that, the market took a beating. Two weeks from the day of the meeting, the Dow Jones average fell by 9 percent. Countless Americans watched helplessly as their IRAs and 401(k)s took a beating. They didn't have the luxury of access to the secret information Dick Durbin exploited.

Six years after Dick Durbin used insider information to protect his investment portfolio, the Occupy Wall Street movement swept across America. The message was focused on income inequality and the special treatment that Washington and Wall Street received. Much of the movement was composed of young, left-leaning Democratic voters.

Washington decided to do something about the animosity aimed at them. On April 4, 2012, President Obama held a ceremony to sign the Stop Trading on Congressional Knowledge (STOCK) Act, a bill that prevents members of Congress from trading stocks based on publicly unavailable information that they gain during the course of their work. It increased transparency and ensured that information regarding members of Congress and staffers was available in an online, searchable database that would be easily accessible to the public.

The ceremony for the bill signing was highly publicized, and President Obama invited eight members of Congress and Vice President Biden to attend. The president walked into the South Court Auditorium of the Eisenhower Executive Office Building smiling. He declared that the bill shows that "when an idea is right . . . we can still accomplish something on behalf of the American people and . . . make our government and our country stronger." He then spoke of fairness and equality, before finally signing the bill into law.

The STOCK Act was a perfect way to calm the political climate in the country, and the president and members of Congress used it as an opportunity to show that they were doing something to put an end to insider trading. But in the end, it was all just a facade.

One week before the law was to go into effect, Congress rushed to gut the key provision of the STOCK Act that would require the records to be accessible online for the public to examine. The provision would have mandated more transparency for members and staffers of Congress and help American citizens and journalists find out if their members were engaging in cronyism. But without any debate, through a fast-track procedure called unanimous consent, Congress removed the key provision in about thirty seconds. They claimed it was necessary for the security of their financial records, but the truth is that it was about protecting them from scrutiny. They're insulating themselves from the public scrutiny that they deserve.

Washington politicians insulate themselves from the American people, and their experience is entirely different from what most of America is going through. While most Americans struggle financially, members of Congress are doing just fine. The median net worth of members of Congress is eighteen times that of average Americans.[16] Since the Great Recession began in 2007, Americans have seen their wealth decrease by 40 percent, but if you look at the bank account of members of Congress, you'd question whether there even was a recession.[17] Since 2007, members of Congress have seen their net worth jump by almost 30 percent.[18] This just shows how disconnected from reality Washington is. While Americans' savings were diminishing and their homes were going into foreclosure, Washington was getting wealthier. How can members of Congress honestly understand the struggles of the American people and represent them if they live a life vastly different from the average American's?

Today, being a member of Congress isn't about serving the people; it's about taking advantage of all the perks that go along with being a "public servant" and using their privileged information to become filthy rich. The entire situation raises the question: What kind of people are we attracting to public service? People don't want to run for office to serve America anymore. They want to serve in order to get access to power and line their pockets.

Washington's War on Women

Income inequality has consistently been a hot topic for the past few election cycles and a central issue to President

Obama's administration. In fact, the first piece of legislation that Obama signed into law as president was the Lilly Ledbetter Fair Pay Act of 2009, which aims to make it easier for women to file gender pay discrimination lawsuits. In a presidential proclamation, President Obama urged Americans to join him and his administration in their efforts to achieve pay equality.

Women make up nearly half of our nation's workforce and are primary breadwinners in four in ten American households with children under age eighteen. Yet from boardrooms to classrooms to factory floors, their talent and hard work are not reflected on payrolls.

Apparently Obama doesn't like the pay disparity between men and women in America, but he doesn't mind it when it happens within his own administration.

For example, for the 2013 fiscal year, the Obama White House paid women less than men, with the average annual pay being $65,000 for women and $75,000 for men.

But Obama isn't the only hypocrite in Washington.

Hillary Clinton fancies herself a champion for equal pay in the workforce. Although she publicly advocates for the destruction of the glass ceiling, there clearly seems to have been a glass ceiling in her office when she was a senator: Her female staffers were paid 72 cents for each dollar paid to her male staffers. The average median salary for a female staffer in her office was $40,791.55, whereas her male employees were paid $56,499.93.

The Clinton Foundation has been a vocal proponent of eliminating the pay disparity between male and female workers. In 2014, they released the "No Ceilings: Full Participation Report," which laid out the gender pay gap and determined that there needs to be more work done to close the gap.

"Since 1995, in 70 countries that include about one-third of the world's population, the average gender wage gap narrowed, from 28 percent to 20 percent," notes the report.

"I hope it serves as a wake-up call, and also as a call to action for us all," writes Clinton.

But it turns out that the Clinton Foundation pays men more than women. According to the recent tax forms filed by the foundation, out of the top eleven employees with the highest salaries, eight of them are men. So while Hillary pretends to be an advocate for women's issues and shattering "the glass ceiling," she chooses to have her male employees paid more than her female employees.

Senator Dick Durbin is another politician who has been one of the leading voices fighting against gender-based inequity, yet doesn't mind income inequality in his Senate office.

In 2014, he held a press conference asking his Senate colleagues to join him in supporting the Paycheck Fairness Act, which would allow women to sue their employers for wage discrimination.

"I want to focus on the power of an idea. It is the idea of fairness. It is the idea of fair pay. It is as basic as being an American and believing that people ought to be treated fairly," Durbin said.

Durbin is in favor of this idea of fairness, but not in his own office.

According to the data available for fiscal year 2013, the average female salary in Durbin's office is more than $11,000 less than the average male salary.

Pay inequity is critical and should be stopped by average American business owners, but not for Durbin.

Durbin and the Democratic leadership in the Senate blasted Republicans for not supporting the Paycheck Fairness Act. Meanwhile, if you looked at the staff of the Democratic leadership at the time, not even one of them had a female chief of staff or communications director—two of the highest and often most-well-paid positions in a congressional office.

Yet it is the Senate Democratic leadership and its communications teams that are complaining about income inequity in America. They are waging a war against the Republican Party and business owners by claiming that the GOP and businessmen are the culprits behind the gender income gap. All the while, members of these entirely male-dominated teams are making better salaries than their female counterparts.

They like to point the finger at private enterprise and accuse them of sexism, but when it comes to their own staffs, they are doing the same thing they're decrying. They are not hiring as many women and are not paying them as much as the men in their offices.

The Right of the Elite People to Keep and Bear Arms

President Obama tried during his first term to get Congress to implement tougher gun control measures, but those efforts failed. It was now time to take matters into his own hands.

In January 2013, President Obama circumvented Congress and issued twenty-three executive actions on gun control, successfully eroding the Second Amendment rights of Americans.

His solution to keep mentally ill individuals from killing innocent Americans was to make it difficult for law-abiding citizens to exercise their Second Amendment rights. His efforts are hypocritical, to say the least, considering Obama is surrounded by a team of armed bodyguards twenty-four hours a day.

While President Obama can enjoy the luxury of being protected, he doesn't believe that average Americans should be able to do the same. It's okay for him to have guns protecting his children, but other American parents shouldn't have that same right.

Another politician who has spent much of his career limiting the rights of gun owners while surrounding himself with armed bodyguards is former New York City mayor, and one of the richest men in the world, Michael Bloomberg.

Michael Bloomberg is an anti-gun zealot who wants to make sure that Americans can't defend themselves. Meanwhile, during his time as mayor, he had a security detail made up of former NYPD officers to protect him. But that doesn't matter, because he's Michael Bloomberg, and the rules don't apply to him.

Despite the obvious hypocrisy, Bloomberg decided to create a group called Mayors Against Illegal Guns. The goal of the organization was to scale back right-to-carry laws in America. The controversial organization faced much criticism, as more than fifty mayors who were initially part of the group decided to leave. The reason for abandoning the group? They thought it was too radical.

One such mayor, John Tkazyik of Poughkeepsie, New York, says he thought the mission of the group was to get guns out of the hands of criminals. He quickly realized that Bloomberg's goal is to confiscate all guns from law-abiding citizens.

It appears as though Bloomberg's ideal scenario is, no doubt, to see an America where citizens don't have access to guns—much like Bermuda, where guns are forbidden. However, Bloomberg, who owns a $10 million waterfront estate in Bermuda, surprisingly isn't much of a fan of the gun situation in Bermuda. Bloomberg has received a special exception from the Bermuda government to allow his bodyguards to carry guns when he vacations there.

That's right. Bloomberg hates the idea of you having a gun, but it's okay for him to travel around America and Bermuda with armed guards. Bloomberg's ideal world isn't one where guns are extinct. His ideal world is one in which he can have a gun, but you can't.

Despite having armed guards around him all the time for protection, he made it clear during a speech at the Aspen Institute that minorities shouldn't enjoy the same rights. "It's controversial, but first thing is all of your—95 percent of your murders, and murderers, and murder victims fit one [unintelligible]. You can just take the description, Xerox it, and pass it out to all of the cops. They are male, minorities, 15 to 25. That's true in New York, it's true in virtually every city in America," said Bloomberg. "You've got to get the guns out of the hands of the people getting killed," he continued. "First thing you can do to help that group is to keep them alive."

In the eyes of Michael Bloomberg, gun laws are for the little people—the "male minorities." He sees nothing hypocritical about him walking around with an armed security detail, while also pouring his vast wealth into his new group Everytown for Gun Safety, a group whose mission is to rival the National Rifle Association.

Granted, the threats that Bloomberg and President Obama face must be taken seriously. But they are no more legitimate than the threats faced by an average American. Why is it that Obama and Bloomberg can have an armed security team to go with them to eat, but average Americans can't have protection when they walk home at night from work? Shouldn't the average American woman, who may live in an area with high crime, be able to defend herself the way Bloomberg and Obama can? How about a former rape victim? Shouldn't she be able to carry a gun for protection if she wants to?

What the political elite are doing is pushing for an unequal system where there is a set of rules for the politically well connected and a whole other set of rules for the rest of us.

The freedom to own and carry a gun is a fundamental right for them, but not for us.

CHAPTER 4

Life After Service

The Clintons

As Bill Clinton stood before an audience of thousands at the National Retail Federation's convention in New York City's Javits Center, he smiled. He always loved the adulation of a crowd (and an intern). And basking in the warmth of their applause, he joked, "It makes me feel like I'm president again."

It makes sense that Slick Willy would feel as though he's president again. Clinton and his family are living as lavishly as, if not more lavishly than, they did when he was president. The crowds are still there, stroking his ego and feeding his narcissism, but now it's even better: He gets to take home a $200,000 paycheck just for showing up. Same goes for Hillary–give or take a few tens of thousands of dollars.

In October 2014, the former secretary of state spoke at the University of Nevada about the need to make higher education more affordable. It's a topic that resonates with many of the University of Nevada's students, who have seen tuition triple in the past decade. "Higher education shouldn't be a privilege for those able to afford it," said Clinton. "It should be an opportunity widely available for anybody with the talent, determination and ambition." But by the time Clinton was finished, the university had $225,000 less it could have spent on scholarships and financial aid to low-income students, because it had written a check in that amount to Hillary Clinton for the pleasure of her company. Hillary had initially demanded $300,000 from the university, but she eventually settled for a $225,000 paycheck in exchange for her presence and her diva demands.[1]

Hillary Clinton may not be president yet–but she demands to be treated like one. When she has a speaking engagement, Hillary isn't flying commercial. Hillary demands a private jet as her mode of transportation, specifically a sixteen-passenger Gulfstream G450–valued at $39 million.[2] She also has some rock star demands: a special podium, a presidential teleprompter, and water onstage with lemon wedges. Hummus, diet ginger ale, and crudités must be placed in the green room for Ms. Clinton.[3] And the chair she'll be sitting on at the event has to be just right. She's known for demanding that the chairs have rectangular pillows, and there must be extra rectangular and long pillows kept in the green room backstage. Clinton also has the last word on the choice of scenery, backdrop, and set of the speech.

When it's time for Clinton to retire for the evening, she's

not going back to any hotel suite. Clinton demands to be placed in a presidential suite in a luxury hotel that has been chosen by either herself or her staff.[4]

And, just as a rock star doesn't travel alone, neither does Hillary–she brings her entire entourage. She has aides who travel with her and an advance team who checks out the speech site three days in advance. The aides arrive early to ensure that the podium and the setup of the event are up to Clinton's standards.

Her usual royal demands for speech engagements include first-class round-trip travel for her aides and entourage, and hotel rooms for them as well. Of course, all of the meals, phone charges, and incidentals accrued by her entourage are expected to be covered by the university or whoever is organizing the speech.[5]

The former first lady makes it clear in her contracts that she will not be there longer than ninety minutes and that she must approve of the moderator of the event. No member of the audience can speak to her directly; only the moderator can ask her questions.[6] There cannot be any press coverage or taping of her speech. Although she is using her public status to demand royal accommodations, she refuses to allow for a public record of her remarks.

For Hillary's speech at the University of Nevada, she allowed for a stenographer, but she would not foot the bill. So, the University of Nevada paid $1,250 to a stenographer.[7] Hillary also demanded that no one other than her and her people be granted access to the speech transcript.

At her speaking engagements she also regulates the number of photos taken of her to "50 clicks."[8] Clinton's representatives told the organizers of one event that all of the photos must be "pre-staged" with everyone ready and in place when Clinton arrived to snap the photo "so the secretary isn't waiting for these folks to get their act together."[9] Clinton's people let the organizers know that Hillary doesn't like to wait around for people.

The speaking circuit is an amazing deal for Clinton: She gets paid an astronomical amount of money to talk for a brief period of time and gets treated like a queen. But the deal isn't so great for the clients who want her to speak. One client in particular, the University of California, Los Angeles, recognized this.

UCLA officials wanted to have the former first lady speak at their campus, but were shocked at the price tag. So they asked Clinton if she could take into consideration the fact that UCLA is a public university and give them a discount.

Her answer? Three hundred thousand dollars is her generous "public university rate."[10]

Thanks to their hefty fees and book contracts, and by virtue of being a former president and first lady, the Clintons have been able to amass a fortune. Since 2001, Bill Clinton has been paid more than $100 million for giving speeches to various industries and groups.[11] Not bad, especially for someone whose wife brings in six-figure speaking fees and, like him, book advances of around $15 million per book.

The enormous wealth they have amassed has helped land the Clintons two beautiful homes: a $5 million brick Geor-

gian home in Washington and a $1.8 million home in Chap-
paqua, New York. And when they need a vacation from their
lucrative gigs they head to the Hamptons for a few weeks,
where they have been known to rent a nine-thousand-square-
foot eight-bedroom home owned by real estate developer Elie
Hirschfeld.[12]

How much do they shell out for their annual brief vacation
to the Hamptons? $200,000.[13]

With the amount of cash and perks that the Clintons—and
other former first families—are able to pull for speeches and
books, you would think that they could live quite well without any taxpayer assistance. But that's only if you haven't
heard of an obscure piece of legislation passed way back in
1958 called the Former Presidents Act.

Before 1958, when a president left office, he didn't receive
a pension or government subsidy. But the well-publicized financial difficulties of former president Harry S. Truman
prompted Congress to make sure former presidents wouldn't
go broke. This probably made sense in an era before $15 mil-
lion book deals were handed out for boring books like Hillary Clinton's *Hard Choices.*

The result, however, is that more than five decades later,
your tax dollars are still footing the bills for families like
the Clintons. In 2012 alone, the U.S. government gave $3.7
million to former presidents for "suitable" office space, security, telephones, health benefits, personnel benefits, printing
costs, cable television, consulting services, travel expenses,
and annual pensions of $200,000.[14] Outgoing presidents
(and vice presidents) even receive extra money in the first six

months after leaving office–up to $1.5 million–in "transi-
tion expenses."

In 2014, President Bill Clinton's wife, Hillary, told ABC's
Diane Sawyer that when she and her husband left the White
House, they were "dead broke." The comment not only
showed how out of touch Clinton is; it was also factually inac-
curate. Thanks to the taxpayer, it's impossible for an outgo-
ing president to be "dead broke."

One of the places where taxpayer dollars go is to Bill Clinton's office, which is located on the top floor of a building in
New York. In 2013, the taxpayers gave the former president
$414,380 just so that he could pay the rent on his luxurious
office space overlooking parts of Manhattan.[15] That's about
$388,000 more per year in federally subsidized real estate
assistance than low-income Americans receive from Section
Eight. One wonders if any of them think about what Cary
Grant told David Niven in *The Bishop's Wife*: "That big roof
could make so many little roofs."

Taxpayer dollars also go to chauffeuring the former first
lady around. Speaking in 2014 before the National Automo-
bile Dealers Association conference in New Orleans, Hillary
confessed: "The last time I actually drove a car myself was
1996."

Clinton is afforded a luxurious life without ever having to
dig into her deep pockets.

One can even argue that the Clintons' living situation is
superior to when they were in the White House. Taxpayers
are still helping maintain their lavish lifestyle, but Bill and

Hillary are now free of the responsibilities that go into being commander in chief and first lady. It's hard to guess what Bill likes better about his new life: The freedom from prying reporters to indulge in his extracurricular interests, if he is so inclined? Or the freedom to cash in from the private sector?

Not only are the taxpayer benefits and earning potential of former presidents great, but they are great for their children as well. Take, for example, the Clintons' daughter, Chelsea Clinton.

In a 2014 interview with *Fast Company,* Chelsea spoke about her career transition from Wall Street to philanthropy, admitting that she "tried really hard to care about things that were very different from my parents. I was curious if I could care about [money] on some fundamental level, and I couldn't. That wasn't the metric of success that I wanted in my life."

Poor thing, right? She tried so hard to care about money but just couldn't. Perhaps it has something to do with the fact that she has been handed a golden ticket into the millionaires club simply because she's a daughter of a former president.

For example, although NBC continues to lay off qualified journalists, it hired Chelsea in 2011 as a special correspondent for its news division. She didn't have a background in journalism or any broadcast experience, but that is immaterial when you're a former first daughter.

Clinton's career at NBC consisted of fake, pre-scripted, awkward segments that were widely ridiculed, with the *Washington Post* even dubbing her "the most boring person of her era." However, despite Clinton's lack of television talent, and mountains of criticism heaped on NBC, the network kept her on the payroll and doled out a reported $600,000 salary for her. Not bad, huh?[16]

NBC eventually realized that the segments with Chelsea weren't great for ratings, so they used her minimally. When all was said and done, Chelsea made about $26,724 for every minute that she appeared on NBC.

Since the whole being-a-reporter thing didn't work out, Chelsea decided to follow in her parents' lucrative footsteps and join the speaking circuit. Chelsea has never been a government official, nor has she held any public policy position, but that doesn't matter when you're Chelsea Clinton. She reportedly can command up to $75,000 for a single appearance.[17]

In fact, Chelsea is able to get more money for speaking than former secretaries of state Colin Powell and Madeleine Albright, who command $50,000 per speech. They may have more accomplishments and far more impressive résumés than Chelsea, but they're no former first daughter.

Being a Clinton pays so well that Chelsea was able to have a wedding that was estimated to have cost $3.3 million. The blushing bride walked down the aisle at the lavish Astor Courts estate in $250,000 worth of jewelry and had not one but two Vera Wang wedding gowns.[18] The one she walked down the aisle in is estimated to have cost $24,900. The mother of the bride, Hillary, opted for a $15,000 Oscar de la Renta gown. The wedding cake reportedly set them back

$11,000.[19] And after the wedding festivities, when it came time to buy a nest, Chelsea shelled out $10.5 million for a five-thousand-square-foot Gramercy Park apartment.[20]

So, if a former first family can all command so much money on their own, why on earth must taxpayers give any money to them? If the market is such that a former first daughter, with very few accomplishments other than being part of a privileged family, can make $75,000 in ninety minutes for talking, why are we paying for her more prominent parents' bills, travel accommodations, office space, and more?

Revolving Door

Life after political office is also an awfully lucrative one for legislators. Whereas once upon a time members of Congress would leave their jobs as public servants and return to simple lives, working on their farms or in their shops, nowadays lawmakers leave the Capitol and head straight to K Street. In K Street's lobbying shops, they can collect nice checks without having to worry about those annoying congressional ethics and disclosure limitations. Even if you lose a humiliating election or endure a career-crushing scandal, you're almost guaranteed a comfy and lucrative gig as a lobbyist.

For example, in 2010, the then senator Chris Dodd was facing a tough reelection. His ethically questionable involvement in Countrywide Financial's VIP program was making headlines. Countrywide executives had wanted influence on Capitol Hill, so they had decided to purchase it by giving out preferential treatment to Senator Dodd, Capitol Hill staffers, government employees, and almost a dozen other lawmakers. Dodd and several other government employees were given lower loan rates by Countrywide in exchange for the company having some allies on Capitol Hill. Dodd and his wife, Jackie, were knowingly part of the VIP program, which helped them save thousands of dollars on two properties they financed.

The story captured the attention of both the press and Dodd's constituents back home, driving his poll numbers down. It wasn't long before it became clear to Dodd and the Democratic Party that he was not going to recover from the scandal. So, after thirty-six years in Congress, the former political star scheduled a press conference to announce that he was retiring from Congress.

One would think the scandal would damage Dodd's ability to seek employment elsewhere. But a scandal that might have sent the average citizen to prison was just a minor bump in the career of Chris Dodd. In Washington, D.C., where failing upward seems to be a common occurrence, Dodd is now more powerful and wealthier than ever.

The next time you watch the Academy Awards, look for Dodd's big head of white hair inside Hollywood's Dolby Theatre. Dodd now spends his time walking down the red carpet at the Oscars, schmoozing with George Clooney, Kevin Spacey, and every other A-list celebrity you can think of, and taking in a $3.3 million annual salary.[21] He is the chairman and CEO of the Motion Picture Association of America.

Senator Dodd's story is a familiar one in Washington. At

the time of his political fall, the MPAA was experiencing a difficult year due to online piracy and the changing entertainment landscape. It was looking for help from someone on Capitol Hill, and it didn't matter whether that person had been entangled in a scandal.

Dodd fit that bill perfectly. He had clocked in a considerable amount of time on Capitol Hill. He had developed relationships with powerful people that the MPAA could benefit from. And he knew he would have no trouble exploiting those lucrative "public servant" chips.

Like her husband, Chris Dodd's wife, Jackie, is a perfect example of the revolving door in Washington. The senator first met Jackie when she was a congressional aide. She later left the Hill for the private sector and eventually became the founder and chief executive of her own consulting firm, Clegg International Consultants. Today, Jackie walks down Hollywood red carpets in the dresses of Felix Alonso, who dressed four generations of Kennedys and is known for dressing Washington's diplomats, ambassadors, and elites.

Working on Capitol Hill pays off, for both former staffers like Jackie and former members of Congress like her husband. Once they've paid a few dues—and made a few influential friends—on Capitol Hill, they cash in on their connections in exchange for incredible salaries. Even relatively junior members of Congress can expect to make an annual salary of about $700,000 on K Street. The Center for Responsive Politics found that 285 former members of Congress now work as lobbyists.

Meanwhile, many of these members are still receiving

pensions from taxpayers. There are 617 members of Congress receiving pensions. In 2013, 367 were receiving an average of $71,664, while another 250 were receiving $42,048. Senator Dodd is estimated to have a federal pension of about $125,500.[22]

In short, being a public servant in Washington is no longer a sacrifice, but a one-way ticket to becoming a millionaire—with a big boost from K Street and an assist from the hard-earned dollars of the American taxpayer.

Anthony Weiner

In May 2011, then congressman Anthony Weiner sent out a tweet to a woman in Washington that linked to a photo of him in his underwear. The congressman immediately deleted the tweet, but not before some of his Twitter followers saw it. He spent the following few days appearing on various cable news shows lying.

Weiner went on CNN and MSNBC and claimed that he couldn't "say with certitude" whether the photo was of him. His defense was that his account had been hacked and that he, in fact, was a "victim." But it was only a matter of time before women started appearing in the media to discuss their online relationships with Weiner, forcing him to admit that his account hadn't been hacked and that he had exchanged explicit photos with six women.

Things got even messier when one of the women, Lisa Weiss, came forward. She claimed that she had carried on a nine-month relationship with Weiner and that he had used government resources to facilitate his online and telephone relationship with her. He reportedly would use government phones, paid for by taxpayers, to carry on his phone-sex conversations with Weiss.

With mounting pressure from his Democratic colleagues to resign, Weiner finally threw in the towel. He left his Capitol Hill office in disgrace. He had embarrassed himself and betrayed the people he promised to work for.

But like so many other members of Congress who left in shame, Weiner shut the door of his office knowing he'd do just fine financially. In Washington, it doesn't matter if you humiliate yourself and betray the people you work for—you still end up walking away with a pretty sweet deal.

When Weiner turns sixty-two, he will be able to collect a pension of up to $46,000 a year.[23] He will also likely be eligible to cash in his congressional Thrift Savings Plan. The plan gives members a 5 percent match of their salary—paid for by taxpayers. Assuming Weiner invested the maximum in it, he left office with more than $200,000 in the account. So while he betrayed his bosses (taxpayers) and left office in disgrace, he won't ever have to worry too much about paying his bills. Thank you, American taxpayer! The former congressman will also still have access to the congressional gym—where he took some of his now infamous nude photos—as well as free parking in the congressional parking lot for life and access to the House floor.

You may be thinking that he should get these benefits. After all, the poor guy is unemployable now, right? Wrong.

After leaving office in disgrace, Anthony Weiner got a

job in public relations. I'm not kidding. The crisis communications firm MWW hired the one guy in America who should never give advice on navigating a scandal. It's likely, though, that he got the PR gig not because of his great public relations skills, but rather because of his connections. The founder of MWW is Michael Kempner, who was also the national finance cochairman for Hillary Clinton's 2008 presidential campaign and her top bundler. Weiner's wife, Huma Abedin, is, of course, a longtime adviser to Hillary Clinton.

It just goes to show that in Washington, D.C., one can only fail upward.

Jesse Jackson Jr.

Many of these great benefits at the expense of taxpayers even apply to members of Congress who are currently serving time in prison.

Not too long ago, former congressman Jesse Jackson Jr. was fighting for a higher minimum wage and social justice. He had his heart set on the Senate seat that Barack Obama was vacating for the White House. He was telling everyone and anyone that he should be Obama's successor. The man in charge of filling that seat was Illinois governor Rob Blagojevich.

Jackson's friend and supporter Raghuveer Nayak reached out to Blagojevich and told him he would give a large donation to the governor's campaign in exchange for appointing Jackson. After the FBI found out, Blagojevich ended up being sentenced to fourteen years in prison for leveraging his political power in the deal. Jackson denied having any knowledge of it and was not charged in the case.

Although Jackson didn't serve any time for his involvement in the deal, his reputation was clearly damaged. And in 2013, his reputation went from damaged to irreparable. Jackson was prosecuted for spending $750,000 from his campaign on personal items, and his wife, Sandi, was prosecuted for failing to report thousands in income from their tax returns. The congressman was sentenced to thirty months in prison, and Sandi was sentenced to twelve months.

With money from his campaign, Jackson and his wife had been living the high life. For example, Jackson bought a gold-plated Rolex costing over $43,000. He also bought porcelain collector's items, Michael Jackson memorabilia, an Eddie Van Halen guitar, Malcolm X memorabilia, and a cashmere cape.[24] The Jacksons even used campaign funds to buy spa trips, cruise trips, and more than $9,000 worth of children's furniture.

But the Jacksons didn't buy just eccentric and lavish things. They also used the campaign money to buy household basics, including soap, toothpaste, booze, groceries, toys, underwear, and toilet paper. All told, they used campaign money to purchase more than three thousand items for themselves.

When Mrs. Jackson found herself in credit card debt, she used campaign money to help pay it off. First, Jackson's campaign paid his wife's business $36,000. Then, just a few days later, Mrs. Jackson transferred the money from the business's accounts to her personal account and used it to help dig herself out of debt.

The manner in which Jackson conducted himself while in office was a slap in the face to his constituents, whom Jackson purported to represent. But what happened right before he was indicted is equally appalling. As federal prosecutors were preparing to indict him, Jackson suddenly developed a mood disorder. How convenient!

Although Jackson spent seventeen years in Congress and never appeared to have any mood disorder, he apparently developed one right before his indictment. His conveniently timed mood disorder qualified him to receive some pretty nice checks while in prison. Jackson can now receive $8,700 a month from taxpayers for his disability.

Also, despite the fact that he was sentenced to prison, Jackson is eligible for a federal pension of about $45,000 once he is sixty-two years old, as well as the funds from his congressional Thrift Savings Plan.[25] If Jackson invested his money aggressively in the program, he will be able to collect a few hundred thousand dollars.

The moral of the story? Even if you betray your constituents, and/or go to jail, the taxpayer will always be there for you.

Lois Lerner

In 2013, it was revealed that the Internal Revenue Service had selectively scrutinized the applications of tea party groups applying for tax-exempt status. During that time, Lois Lerner was the head of the tax-exempt division, which was tasked with applying additional scrutiny if its members received an application that used words such as "tea party" or "patriot." Lerner's division even released confidential applications from conservative groups to the left-leaning news site ProPublica in 2012.

Although her division, and the IRS in general, is supposed to be run by nonpartisan individuals, emails released by the House Ways and Means Committee show that Lerner was anything but nonpartisan. In the emails, Lerner refers to conservatives as "crazies" and "assholes."

When Lerner was summoned by the House Committee on Oversight and Reform to testify, she chose not to answer any questions about her division's blatant overreach and targeting of conservative groups. "I have not done anything wrong," she said. "I have not broken any laws. I have not violated any IRS rules or regulations." Lerner then pled the Fifth and deprived Americans of important answers.

Although she's a "public servant," she refused to help taxpayers and investigators uncover who was involved in the potential targeting of President Obama's enemies. And since she refused to speak, the only way for Americans and investigators to get a more thorough understanding of the targeting of Americans would be to look through her emails.

Except, there was a problem.

The Internal Revenue Service informed congressional investigators that Lerner's emails during the two years of targeting of conservatives had vanished! Lerner's computer apparently crashed in 2011. Among the lost data were the emails from five junior employees at the IRS who were involved in the targeting of conservative groups. Convenient.

During the months-long investigation, Lerner was placed on paid administrative leave. She was still able to collect her $177,000 salary from the taxpayers–the very people she targeted. The American taxpayer paid for her comfy life, while she refused to be held accountable for her actions.

Any ordinary American who worked at a company and targeted her own boss–the person who writes the checks– would be kicked to the curb. But in Washington there aren't consequences for top government officials who target the people who pay their salary. When Lerner eventually retired in September 2013, she was able to retire comfortably. She is currently living in her $2.4 million–plus home in Maryland. And the taxpayer remains on the hook–reportedly shelling out $100,000 annually for Lois Lerner's pension.

Only in Washington can you bite the hand that feeds you, and still get fed.

Emanuel, Orszag, and Gibbs

The taxpayers' generosity extends to all federal workers, including White House staff. But why? While White House staffers are collecting money from taxpayers, they are amassing contacts they can then use to create fortunes. At a time when we're $18 trillion in debt, it makes little sense for taxpayers to give generous benefits to people who can turn around and easily amass fortunes larger than the average American would ever dream of.

We refer to White House staffers as "public servants," yet

they're anything but servants. If anything, they're "the chosen ones" who have been afforded the opportunity to become millionaires through two popular career routes after the White House, Wall Street and K Street, where they receive huge salaries in exchange for tapping into their contacts and relationships.

Take, for example, the former Clinton aide Rahm Emanuel, who left the White House in 1998. Like many White House staffers before him, he went to the financial sector, joining Wasserstein Perella & Co. as a managing director. Emanuel didn't have a background in finance, and he certainly didn't have the credentials to land such a high-paying gig. But that didn't matter, because a former White House staffer's phone book is more important to prospective employees than any degree or otherwise relevant experience.

The *Chicago Sun-Times* asked Emanuel to describe what he did. He said, "I was what was considered, at that time, although I don't think this is really interesting, relationship banking, and that's what I did."

Emanuel was in the "relationship banking" industry for about two and a half years. How much did Emanuel make for his brief tenure? $18.5 million.

Emanuel spent those two and half years working with the Democratic Party's biggest financial supporters. He was able to land clients and seal deals because of the people he had encountered during his time at the White House.

For example, Emanuel met Bernard Schwartz during his time working for the White House. Schwartz was the single biggest donor during the Clinton years. He had such a close relationship with the Clintons that when he turned seventy-one years old, he celebrated his birthday at the White House.

When Emanuel left the White House, he called up Schwartz, who, at the time, was the head of Loral Space & Communications. Schwartz told Emanuel to meet him at his office in New York to talk. Schwartz ended up hiring Emanuel and his new firm, Wasserstein Perella & Co.[26]

"He knew a lot of high-level people in U.S. corporations, and they respected him," Schwartz told the *Chicago Tribune,* when asked why he hired Emanuel. "So he can get to the high level of corporations to present ideas. And that's half the battle: to get to the right people, so you don't waste a lot of time."

Schwartz is hardly the only person who was willing to fork up tons of money to pay for Emanuel's contacts. And Emanuel isn't the only former White House staffer in the business of influence peddling. Peter Orszag, Obama's budget director, made $196,700 as a public servant. Then he left his position to make $3.1 million in taxable income at Citigroup.

These public servants also get paid enormous amounts just to speak. For example, Obama's former political adviser, David Plouffe, was paid to speak at an event in Azerbaijan. He was given $50,000.[27]

The list of former White House staffers cashing in on their contacts and White House access is endless. Former White House press secretary Robert Gibbs left the White House in 2011, and by 2013 he had made $2 million in speeches alone. Former deputy campaign manager Stephanie Cutter created a consulting group, Precision Strategies, and landed a contract with CNN as cohost of *Crossfire.* Plouffe joined the car-sharing company Uber as a senior vice president. Former campaign manager Jim Messina founded the Messina Group, a consulting firm. Former speechwriter Jon Favreau went on to form a political consulting firm called Fenway Strategies with former National Security Council spokesperson Tommy Vietor.

Being a public servant seems more like a golden ticket to wealth than like service. There is no reason why taxpayers should be providing lavish benefits for people who can easily make a pretty penny off their public service. It doesn't even matter if you're awful at your job. In Washington, one only fails upward. There is never really a true fall from grace. Politicians who are terrible at their jobs, embarrass their constituents, or abuse the system always have a comfy retirement system or a Rolodex of important contacts to fall back on. There seem to be no consequences for the actions of people, except simply more money, more notoriety, and a new job.

Only in America?

No, only in Washington.

CHAPTER 5

Family Affairs

W hen the founding fathers gathered in Philadelphia in the summer of 1787 to draft our nation's
Constitution, they fiercely and stubbornly argued over many questions that divided big states from small
states, industrialists from agrarians, and North from South.
But there was one principle on which every delegate to the
convention agreed: In the United States, there would be no
nobility. No dukes, earls, or barons. No hereditary titles or
privileges of any kind, for any class. And so it was neither
surprising nor controversial that the first article of the Constitution they created included the following decree: "No
Title of Nobility shall be granted by the United States."

Today in Washington, D.C., dynasties such as the Clintons
and Bushes barely raise an eyebrow. Privileges and perks for
the family members of congresspeople are taken for granted.

Spouses of cabinet secretaries receive special treatment, and nepotism is the norm.

This most un-American of phenomena is so widespread that reporting it isn't hard; the hard part is determining which of the countless examples to write about. It's like writing about the unhealthy items on Taco Bell's menu: so many to choose from.

In this chapter, I present a narrowed-down list of Washington's family-first abuses of power. In no particular order, here are nine of the most egregious instances of Versailles-style nepotism in a city named for the general and gentleman who presided at the Constitutional Convention that desired no titles of nobility in the United States.

1. Harry Reid

In 2002, Senator Harry Reid proposed a Nevada land bill called the Clark County Conservation of Public Land and Natural Resources Act. It was not a title that would raise an alarm in the capital's ideological wars. It was unlikely to anger the NRA, EMILY's List, or the host of other interest groups that make so much noise and attract so much attention in Washington.

The Clark County bill had the support of Nevada's other senator–Republican John Ensign–and was signed into law by President George W. Bush in November 2002. Both before and after the bill's passage, Reid praised it as a great piece of legislation that would promote economic opportunity and growth in Nevada.

Sounds good, right?

What Reid failed to mention was that the bill would also promote economic opportunity and growth for one specific family in Nevada: the Reid family. Real estate developers and corporations—who stood to make a fortune off the bill—were paying hundreds of thousands of dollars in lobbying fees to the law firm that employs Reid's sons.[1] In addition, Reid's sons represented the local governments that benefited the most from the bill—Las Vegas, Henderson, and North Las Vegas.

It gets even worse. The Howard Hughes Corporation was also a huge beneficiary of the legislation. Before the bill passed, the corporation paid $300,000 to a consulting firm owned by Steven Barringer—Harry Reid's son-in-law.[2]

This practice of relatives of congresspeople lobbying Congress is unethical but not illegal. Lobbying firms fork over large sums of money to congressional leaders' relatives all the time. At least twenty-eight members of Congress have close family members who lobby or consult for firms and clients who pay them in part because of the special access they'll get.[3]

According to the *Los Angeles Times,* "Harry Reid is in a class by himself." Over a recent four-year period, the firms of his sons and son-in-law have made "more than $2 million in lobbying fees from special interests that were represented by the kids and helped by the senator in Washington."

But Reid's questionable conduct does not stop there. In 2011, his son Josh wanted to be city attorney in Henderson, Nevada (if you remember, one of the cities that benefited from Reid's 2002 land bill). There was just one little problem—Josh didn't meet the requirements for the $199,471 job.[4]

The job posting said that no candidate would be considered unless he or she had ten years of experience as an attorney and at least five years' experience with a public agency.[5] Josh met neither qualification. But when your father is a powerful member of Congress, there's no problem that Dad can't fix with a few phone calls.

Harry Reid made a call to the mayor, Andy Hafen, who was a friend of Reid's. Hafen's daughter, Tessa, was Reid's former spokeswoman and also worked for Reid's son Rory.[6] It was like a Nevada version of *Downton Abbey*.

Reid told Hafen that he "would find nobody more academically qualified than Josh."[7] He also called Councilwoman Kathleen Vermillion to lobby on his son's behalf. After those calls—surprise!—the City of Henderson Human Resources Department decided to change the requirements. Now no previous work for a public agency would be required, and the candidate would need only eight years' experience as an attorney—which just happened to be a bar low enough for Josh Reid to meet.

When Josh Reid was, predictably, hired—over five other semifinalists, all of whom met the original requirements—city officials maintained that they weren't swayed by the fact that Harry Reid had called them. I'm sure the local politicians had no concerns about getting on the bad side of one of the most influential members of Congress. I'm sure they didn't consider their need for a friend in Congress to help them secure federal dollars for their projects. I'm sure they didn't ask themselves, "Why create an enemy out of the most powerful Democrat in our state?"

Believe it or not, stories of Harry Reid's questionable ethics in the context of his family don't stop there. I could go on and on. But let's end with a little story from that happiest of times, that season of giving–Christmastime.

In 2013 and 2014, Harry Reid had to give Christmas gifts to staff and supporters for the holiday. And, at the time, Reid's twenty-three-year-old granddaughter, Ryan Elisabeth Reid, had a small start-up jewelry business that needed some help. What a lovely coincidence!

Riding to the rescue of young Ryan, Grandpa Reid decided to kill two birds with one stone. He bought $31,000 worth of jewelry from his granddaughter and gave it to his staffers.[8] But he didn't buy it with his own money. Instead, he bought it with campaign funds and listed it on his expenditures as "holiday gifts."

Curiously, Reid omitted his granddaughter's last name from the expenditure report; "Ryan Elisabeth Reid" became "Ryan Elisabeth." He apparently had hoped that no one would catch on to the fact that he had put money from his campaign into the pockets of his granddaughter.

It pays to be a Reid. Literally.

2. Joe Biden

In April 2014, violence erupted in Kiev between pro-Russian separatists and Ukrainian nationalists. At the center of the conflict was natural gas, with Ukraine accusing Russia of hiking gas prices. It was the kind of complicated geopolitical crisis that receives the attention of the world's finest foreign policy minds. And Joe Biden's.

Vice President Biden has been wrong, as Defense Secretary Robert Gates once wrote, about "nearly every major foreign policy and national security issue over the past four decades." Nevertheless, the White House put Biden at the helm of solving the energy situation in Ukraine by sending him to offer advice to Ukrainians on how the United States could assist them in expanding their production of natural gas.

One month after the trip, in what may just be an incredibly unbelievable coincidence, Joe Biden's son landed a key position in the Ukrainian gas industry.

You know . . . the industry that is front and center of the Ukrainian crisis.

It was announced that Burisma Holdings, the largest private gas producer in Ukraine, had hired Biden's son Hunter–right in the midst of the Ukrainian crisis. The company also announced that it would hire Devon Archer, a family friend of Secretary of State John Kerry. Archer was the college roommate of Kerry's stepson, Christopher Heinz–the H. J. Heinz Company heir. Archer's job at the gas company is to attract investors from America and expand the company's operations.[9]

The appointment of the vice president's son to the largest private Ukrainian gas company–at a time when the United States is working to help Ukraine become less dependent on Russia for oil–appears awfully suspicious. However, the White House and Biden's spokesperson were quick to assure the media that there was no conflict of interest. Right.

While the White House didn't see any conflict of interest, the rest of the world saw it as a "You scratch my back,
I'll scratch my back" scenario. It appeared as though the vice
president's trip to Kiev was more about securing a position of
employment for his son than about actually doing work.

Nor was this the first time Biden may have used his position and influence to help out Hunter. Thanks to Dad's
cozy relationship with a top executive at MBNA, the giant
credit card company in Biden's home state of Delaware hired
Hunter to a cushy position, from which he was quickly promoted to senior vice president. This was the same MBNA that
paid that top executive, John Cochran, $300,000 in "mov-
ing expenses" after he bought Joe Biden's house for almost
two times what it was worth.[10]

In 2002, Hunter decided to move on to bigger and better
things. With the help of his dad, he became a founding part-
ner at the lobbying firm Oldaker, Biden & Belair. William
Oldaker was Joe Biden's adviser during his unsuccessful
1988 presidential campaign. (Presumably he wasn't the one
who advised Biden to plagiarize a speech from a British
Labour leader.)

During Hunter's time as a lobbyist, one of Dad's friends—
the then senator Barack Obama—helped him out by seeking more than $3.4 million in earmarks for one of Hunter's
clients, St. Xavier University in Chicago.[11] Already beginning his pattern of overpromising and underdelivering (remember hope and change?), Obama ended up securing only
$192,000 for Hunter Biden's client.[12]

By now, you might be thinking that life for Hunter has

been all wine and roses. But if so, you'd be forgetting about the cocaine.

When Hunter was a young man, he was caught in a drug-related incident that later almost kept him out of the navy. But the navy gave Hunter a waiver for the incident. (It also gave him an age waiver and selected him for a prestigious program for people whose special skills compensate for their lack of military experience—even though it's unclear what Hunter's special skills were, other than being really good at getting military waivers.)

But, alas, Hunter Biden's drug problems weren't entirely behind him. In 2014, just one month after he joined the navy, he was kicked out for testing positive for cocaine. Now, who could have possibly seen that coming?

At that point, if Hunter's last name had not been Biden, one would have expected the Connecticut Bar Association to refuse to review his law license. After all, lawyers are dangerous enough when they're not running around hopped up on cocaine. But when asked about the incident, the president of the CBA, Mark Dubois, said that although they take information about the misbehavior of lawyers very seriously, they "have to be judicious about starting the process."[13]

Translation: We're not looking into it.

3. Nancy Pelosi

For the past decade, Congresswoman Nancy Pelosi has been one of the biggest, most vocal supporters of a light-rail project in California, working to secure $1 billion to help create the railway. Of course, she might have worked so hard for this project just because she really, really likes trains. But there's another possibility—one that becomes quite glaring when you follow the advice of Deep Throat to Woodward and Bernstein: "Follow the money."

Just as the transcontinental railroad spiked the value of land on its path, the light-rail project in California has helped increase the value of real estate along its route. In 2010, a company called Salesforce bought much of that land for around $270 million.[14] Then, after Pelosi's project took off, Salesforce sold the land for an undisclosed amount to the NBA's Golden State Warriors, who paid, in their own words, "a very pretty penny."

So what does Salesforce have to do with Nancy Pelosi? Well, first of all, its CEO, Marc Benioff, is a major Democratic donor. But even more noteworthy is that a major investor in Salesforce is Paul Pelosi, the congresswoman's husband. He has between $500,000 and $1 million invested in the company, which has been an enormous beneficiary of the light-rail subsidies that Nancy Pelosi worked tirelessly to secure.[15]

4. Eric Holder

The preferential treatment of family members applies not just to members of Congress but also to the relatives of the U.S. attorney general.

Between 2009 and 2011, the U.S. Bureau of Alcohol, Tobacco, Firearms, and Explosives—a division of the Justice Department—ran an operation called Fast and Furious. It intentionally allowed firearms to get into the hands of Mexican drug cartels. The thinking was that the ATF would track these firearms, which would eventually lead its officers to key Mexican drug dealers so that they could arrest them. However, the ATF lost track of approximately 1,400 guns.

The guns ended up being found at crime scenes in the United States and in Mexico. The operation remained a secret to the public until the guns were found at the Arizona site where Customs and Border Protection agent Brian Terry was killed. In December 2010, Terry was on patrol when gunfire began. During the fight, Terry was killed. After the fight, two AK-47 assault rifles were recovered from the scene. Both of the guns were sold through Operation Fast and Furious.

Justice Department officials in D.C. tried to distance themselves from the operation. They claimed not to have known about the operation, or to have known about it too late to stop it. In May 2011, Attorney General Eric Holder testified to the House Judiciary Committee that he had heard of the operation only a few weeks prior to testifying. But documents show that Holder had known about the operation for almost a year, not for a few weeks, as he had claimed. Memos regarding the gun-running operation were addressed to Holder going back to July 2010.[16]

The House committee requested documents regarding the botched operation in order to fully understand who knew what about it, why it was able to continue for so long, and what the circumstances were that led to the death of Brian Terry.

Holder refused to hand over the materials and, asserting executive privilege, President Obama backed his buddy up. Thanks to Obama, Holder no longer had to disclose the documents.

While it is noteworthy that the White House chose to invoke executive privilege over documents that don't involve communications with the White House, it is not unprecedented. But what is unprecedented is that the executive privilege was given to Eric Holder's wife, Sharon Malone.

Malone isn't a government employee. She's a private physician. Yet President Obama invoked executive privilege for email correspondence between Holder and Malone. The president also invoked executive privilege for communications between Holder and his mother.[17]

What did Holder's wife and mother have to do with Operation Fast and Furious? Who knows. But what we do know is that the chance of executive privilege being extended to ordinary citizens is pretty slim—unless you're the wife or mother of a cabinet official. In that case, no problem!

5. Runts and Reporters

The nepotism in Washington also extends to the media. Having a famous parent in Washington has now become a one-way ticket to a high-paying job in journalism.

Luke Russert was twenty-two years old and had been out of college for just a few months when NBC hired him to cover the 2008 presidential election. Did young Luke have any experience in television? No. But that didn't matter, because he was the son of late journalist Tim Russert and journalist Maureen Orth. As NBC's Tom Brokaw explained, "Luke, in a way, has been preparing for this moment all his life. He grew up in the loving care of two world-class journalists."[18]

Only in Washington are "Mom" and "Dad" considered relevant job experiences on a résumé.

When Luke was hired, he addressed the criticism regarding his lack of experience. "I had twenty-two years of advice from my father," said Luke, "and I still get advice from my mother every day." He added, "If you ask if I'm ready to do it, I've been answering their questions for that amount of time. I can definitely take from what they asked me." (It was this kind of eloquence that Luke brought to the network of Brinkley and Brokaw.)

To be sure, the children of reporters can sometimes make for excellent journalists. Chris Wallace comes to mind. But the problem with Luke Russert is that he's bad at his job. He's a mediocre journalist with less-than-mediocre skills on camera, who was hired for the wrong reasons, promoted to congressional correspondent over far more qualified colleagues, and then, in September 2014, given a gig on *Meet the Press* that came with an extra, and completely undeserved, $500,000.[19]

Luke Russert wasn't the first person hired by MSNBC simply because he or she was the spawn of the political elite. In 2011, the network hired as a political analyst a young art history major with little experience working in politics. Her name was Meghan McCain. Two years later, MSNBC hired Abby Huntsman, Jon Huntsman's daughter, as a cohost of MSNBC's daytime show *The Cycle.* Abby's experience rivals that of Meghan McCain–they are both the daughters of men who lost presidential campaigns.

I know what you're thinking: Who cares who MSNBC hires? No one is watching anyway! But the danger with nepotism in the media is that we continue to prop up people who have never experienced life outside the Beltway. They are so disconnected from the everyday experiences of ordinary Americans that they cannot represent the concerns of the American people in the media and elsewhere. Their perspectives are not fresh and new, but literally inbred. They are the product of an insulated environment in which everyone in Washington understands one another, but can't understand the American people. And it's not even their fault. After all, how can we expect the children of power players to fairly cover the conduct of power players?

Democrats and the ruling elite in Washington constantly preach about the unfairness of the 1 percent having more than the 99 percent. They are constantly trying to implement policies to level the playing field. However, when it comes to inside the Beltway, it's fine for a kid with no experience to land a high-paying job covering her dad's buddies in Washington. It's perfectly fine for a congressman's kid to become a lobbyist and cash in on his dad's connections. Outside of Washington, D.C., that would be considered unsavory and downright corruption. But in Washington, D.C., that's just how it works. It's life!

6. Joe Manchin

Why would a university alter transcripts to make it look like someone had a degree she didn't earn? Well, you'd have to ask the folks at West Virginia University, because that's exactly what they did for Senator Joe Manchin's daughter.

Heather Bresch was job hunting. But as the daughter of Joe Manchin, then a West Virginia state senator, her job search wasn't much like the job searches of millions of ordinary Americans in the past decade or so of slow economic growth. She found a job with relative ease, shortly after her father attended a college basketball game.

At the game, Manchin ran into Milan Puskar, the cofounder of Mylan, the world's third-largest generic drug company. Puskar was a contributor to Manchin's campaigns, and after Manchin told Puskar about his daughter's need for a job, Heather was hired on at Mylan. But all was not as it seemed.

In her résumé, Heather had completely fabricated an MBA degree from West Virginia University. To keep up the facade, the university rewrote her transcripts, adding classes and grades to her record that didn't exist.[20]

Eventually, after it was caught red-handed, the university rescinded the degree. The president of the university resigned, as did other officials. But there was one person who skated by largely unharmed—Senator Joe Manchin's daughter Heather.

This type of scandal would likely bring down most ordinary people, but not Heather. She was appointed president of the company in 2009 and CEO in 2012. That same year, *Fortune* magazine named her one of the most powerful women in business.

7. U.S. Patent Office

By now, we've pretty well established that D.C. bigwigs help close relatives at taxpayer expense. But Deborah Cohn, the commissioner of trademarks for the U.S. Patent and Trademark Office, went even further. She helped her relative's boyfriend.

Even after Cohn helped the boyfriend network and edited his résumé and cover letters for him, he still couldn't land a gig. Undeterred, Cohn used her work email to contact her colleagues' spouses, old friends, and anyone else she could think of to connect him with. But the guy just couldn't get anyone to hire him.

So what's a high-ranking official in the government to do? Cohn decided she was going to just get him a job in her agency.

First, Cohn pressured officials to hire this unqualified boyfriend of her relative for an open position in the U.S. Patent and Trademark Office. But her relative's boyfriend was so unqualified that he didn't get past the first round of screening. The officials in charge of hiring narrowed down the list of more than 700 people to 250 candidates.[21] The boyfriend didn't make the cut.

Cohn intervened again. Despite her relative's boyfriend being clearly ill-equipped, Cohn pushed him through another round of screening. In this round, he finished seventy-fifth out of seventy-six candidates.[22]

But that wasn't going to stop Cohn, who wielded considerable power in the agency. She finally decided to just create a new position for the boyfriend. It didn't matter to Cohn that he was obviously not good enough for a key position in the government. It didn't matter to her that taxpayers would have to spend money paying for the salary of someone who wasn't the best fit for the role. Nothing was going to stop her from—in true Versailles style—bringing a new courier to the king's court.

8. The Clintons' Son-in-Law

Life is pretty good for Marc Mezvinsky, the husband of Chelsea Clinton. Thanks to his powerful mother- and father-in-law, Mezvinsky is able to play around with tons of people's money. A year after Mezvinsky married Chelsea, he and his buddies decided to create the hedge fund EagleVale Partners.

When you're married to someone in the Clinton clan, big financial firms are quick to help you out. For example, right before the launch of the fund, Goldman Sachs organized events to introduce investors to the fund. The events were a hit, attracting standing-room-only crowds.[23]

Within a short period of time, Mezvinsky and his friends were managing $400 million.

But in 2015, the firm lost big. While a firm similar to EagleVale saw a 5.7 percent increase in its fund, Mezvinsky's main fund saw a drop of 3.6 percent. And another smaller fund Mezvinsky organizes dropped by 48 percent in 2014.[24]

Mezvinsky had bet on Greece's economy recovering, but

a radical left-wing party came into control in 2015 and cost the fund tremendous amounts of money.

But the truth is that Mezvinsky's poor track record likely won't prevent people from investing in the fund. Most of the rich people who gave Mezvinsky money are interested in a much bigger investment—access to America's most elite family.

Many of the powerful and wealthy individuals who gave money to Mezvinsky are Democratic donors.

The CEO of Goldman Sachs, Lloyd Blankfein, is a major investor in the fund. His political contributions have gone to Chris Dodd, Al Gore, and of course Hillary Clinton.

Another investor is Marc Lasry, the co-owner of the NBA's Milwaukee Bucks. Lasry used to employ Chelsea Clinton at Avenue Capital Group and, shocker, is a Democratic donor.[25] He hosted a $40,000-per-plate fundraiser at his home in Manhattan for President Obama's reelection campaign.

Adding to the incestuous nature of Washington, Lasry's daughter worked for former Democratic congressman Rahm Emanuel and then went on to work for Obama. In 2013, Lasry was supposed to be nominated as the ambassador of Paris. He withdrew his name from the highly sought-after position after he was linked to an alleged poker ring run by Russian mobsters.

But, in all honesty, these investors aren't really all that concerned about making money right away. If they were, they would go to plenty of other firms that have a much better record than Mezvinsky's.

These wealthy and powerful Democratic donors are

thinking long-term. Yes, they'll lose money with Mezvinsky playing around with it, but when Mezvinsky's mother-in-law is in the White House, that's when they'll really cash in.

9. The Dingells

Our forefathers may have fought a revolution to get away from a monarchy, but America has managed to develop its own dynasty over time–the Dingell dynasty. When it comes to the Dingell family, inheriting a position of power is just part of the family tradition.

John Dingell Sr. was born in 1894. Grover Cleveland was president. The Pullman strike was the story of the year. And a new soda called Coca-Cola was sold in bottles for the first time. That year, more than century ago, is where the Dingell dynasty began.

In 1932, with New York governor Franklin Roosevelt running for president, Dingell was elected to Congress. For the next twenty-two years, he would represent Michigan's Fifteenth Congressional District.

After Dingell died suddenly in 1955, his twenty-nine-year-old son, John Jr., assumed his office, where he stayed for the next sixty years. That adds up to eighty-eight years of Dingells.

When John Dingell Jr. announced in February 2014 that he would be retiring, he said, "I find serving in the House to be obnoxious."[26] Of course, it must not have been that bad, considering that he subjected himself to his taxpayer-funded position for six decades. If it was so painful, why not retire from your position earlier and allow for new people with fresh ideas to run for your position?

Moreover, if he found serving in Congress so obnoxious, then why did he prop up his wife as his successor?

Yes, being in the House of Representatives was so "obnoxious" that Dingell decided to keep with the Dingell dynasty family tradition and hand off his seat to Debbie Dingell. In 2014, she won her husband's congressional seat, thus carrying on the tradition of a more-than-eight-decades-long hold on the seat. And since Debbie is only sixty-two years old, it's possible that the seat will remain in the Dingell family for one hundred years. Not a bad inheritance, huh?

The heir to that inheritance may be John Dingell's son Christopher. He became a state senator at the young age of thirty and now is a judge in the Dingell dynasty congressional district. If Debbie Dingell finds that the job is too "obnoxious" for her—no worries. There is always another Dingell waiting in line for the job.

A merica is no stranger to nepotism. The first American to commit a large public act of nepotism was President John Adams. He made his son John Quincy Adams the U.S. minister to the Netherlands. Today, most children of political dynasties would be jumping for joy if their dad landed them a high-paying, high-profile diplomatic position. John Quincy, however, was anything but happy at this blatant act of nepotism. In fact, he was ashamed that his father had appointed him. He wrote in his diary: "I wish I could have been consulted before [the nomination] was irrevocably made. . . . I rather wish it had not been made at all."[27] Many critics agreed with John Quincy Adams—the appointment was wrong and appeared as a step toward creating a political monarchy.

Thomas Jefferson was also appalled by this act of nepotism and later wrote that "the public will never be made to believe that an appointment of a relative is made on the ground of merit alone, uninfluenced by family views; nor can they ever see with approbation offices, the disposed of which they entrust to their president for public purposes, divided out as family property. Mr Adams degraded himself infinitely on this matter." Unfortunately, John Adams didn't take the advice of Jefferson and, two hundred years later, the appointment of family members to important political positions has gotten out of control in Washington.

Nepotism is dangerous for America because of the high probability of corruption and cover-ups. There is also the issue of fairness: Why should taxpayers sign the checks of privileged people who didn't have to earn their positions? These family appointees didn't have to work for their position or prove themselves worthy; they just had the right bloodline, contacts, and/or name recognition. It goes against everything this country stands for and leads to diminishing confidence on the part of the American people. Jefferson was correct in pointing out that Adams degraded himself, and America, on the issue of nepotism. But today, it isn't just one person who is degrading America—it's all of Washington, D.C.

CHAPTER 6

Narcissism:

Extreme Selfishness, with a Grandiose View of One's Own Talents and a Craving for Admiration[1]

Sheila Jackson Antoinette

Sheila Jackson Lee was mad. *Verrrrrrrry* mad. "I am a queen!" the Texas congresswoman barked at her helpless staffer. "And I demand to be treated like a queen!"

Jackson Lee had just rented a car to take her to the Faith and Politics Institute Event. Only after renting the car did she learn that another member of Congress, who was attending the same event, didn't have to rent a car. He was being driven to the event by a member of Faith and Politics, the group organizing the conference.

The folks at Faith and Politics were likely unaware of the self-important demands that Jackson Lee constantly makes on those around her. But outbursts like the one Jackson Lee was having over her car situation were—and remain—the norm.[2] Jackson Lee may be a public "servant" in title, but she expects to be treated like royalty. And when you've got a staff, paid for by taxpayers, you can ensure that you get only the best treatment.

For example, Jackson Lee is known to designate one of her Capitol Hill staffers as her driver to pick her up every morning. She sometimes has two drivers—one car for her and the other car for her bags.

Oh, and the kicker? Sheila Jackson Lee lives only one block away from her Capitol Hill office.[3]

Any ordinary citizen who had to pay for daily private car service out of her own pocket would likely see this as an incredible waste of money. However, Jackson Lee doesn't seem to worry about wasting money, because it's not her money—it's yours.

Jackson Lee's preference for being chauffeured in her royal chariot doesn't stop with her morning commute. If she needs to go from one Capitol Hill office building to another, she doesn't walk.[4] Walking across the street is for peasants. She has one of her drivers transport her.

And Jackson Lee's driver doesn't just pick her up, drop her off, and move on to more important matters. Her drivers are known to wait for hours for her. All the while her car is idling.

So, if you have to walk a block, make a staffer drive you. And if you have an important meeting, make 'em wait—even if the person waiting is a cabinet secretary.

When the then secretary of transportation Ray LaHood was scheduled to meet with Jackson Lee, he was forced to wait an hour and a half for her.[5] Meanwhile, Jackson Lee was on the House floor, waiting for her chance to appear before C-SPAN cameras. It didn't matter to her that LaHood was waiting in her office to talk to her about issues important to her constituents. On Capitol Hill, television time takes precedence over getting work done.

It's Jackson Lee's world. We're just living in it. And paying for it.

State of the Union

Each year the president gives a speech to the American people outlining the state of the union. The practice originally started as an opportunity for the president to deliver a message to Congress—as required by the Constitution—and then turned into an opportunity for the president to address the American people.

But the State of the Union address is now something else entirely. It is a show. It is a farce. It is an empty and pompous ritual for the status-obsessed D.C. elite.

When the event begins, the national media stop everything they're doing to show members of Congress and the president's cabinet walk in, in the same way that the media wait for George Clooney and his wife to exit their limo and step onto the red carpet at a Hollywood premiere. For one night a year, the aisle from the back of Congress to its front becomes like the runway of the Oscars, and our political reporters become like Melissa Rivers, Carson Daly, and TMZ.

What should be a serious moment for our government has become akin to the Grammys. For example, in 2015, a Twitter Mirror was installed. The "mirror," which has become a staple at Hollywood red carpet events, is now being used by the first lady, her guests, and the rest of the ego-obsessed D.C. elite and celebrities to take self-portraits. They stand in front of the tablet with a filigree frame on the wall, pose, approve the photo, and send it out into the Twitterverse.

The State of the Union could and should be an opportunity for the president to speak directly to the American people with candor and substance, but it is just another self-serving event for Washington. The fact that the address is clearly off-putting to average Americans—who tune out in higher numbers each year—is of no concern to those inside the Beltway. Regardless of the ratings, for many members the State of the Union is their time to shine.

The whole spectacle is a favorite among the D.C. elite, but particularly among the members of Congress who don't usually get national media attention. They don't care if their constituents hear about new ideas that could improve their lives and their neighborhoods. These members of Congress care mostly about getting their faces on national television so they can appear powerful and important.

Case in point: Representative Eliot Engel.

Engel's claim to fame isn't being a great congressman who gets work done. Rather, he is famous for being obsessed with getting the best seat at the State of the Union speech.[6] He wants oh-so-badly to be perceived as important that it's almost comedic.

Every year, the day that the president delivers his annual State of the Union speech, Engel stakes out the aisle seat that is best positioned to give him the most visibility on national television. He makes sure the seat is one the president walks past during the entrance and exit processions through the House chamber. Engel wants the cameras on him, and he wants to be seen shaking the president's hand. As a rank-and-file legislator outside of the House leadership teams, he uses this moment to elevate his profile and make people think he is part of "the club."

The quality that determines your status in Washington is whether you have relationships with important people in the Beltway. So it's no surprise that Engel wants to ensure that what comes through the television screen on the night of the State of the Union is that he's powerful and connected.

Seats are given out on a first-come, first-served basis. The president delivers his speech at nine P.M. EST. So every year since he was elected in 1989, Engel has arrived almost twelve hours before the speech is made to get his seat. He lays something down to claim his seat and watches it for the rest of the day to ensure no other members of Congress take it.[7]

When asked why he has become an "aisle hog," he said: "I found that when I did it initially, which was a total fluke, I found people in my district coming up to me saying, 'I saw you on TV, you were great, I saw you with the president.' "[8]

It's for the constituents. Right.

It's more likely that Engel is just like most people in D.C.– obsessed with appearing powerful, stroking his ego, and strengthening his "brand."

Unsurprisingly, Congresswoman (or queen?) Sheila Jackson Lee is also part of the State of the Union seat warmers club. When asked by the *National Journal* why she insists on staking out an aisle seat each year, she claimed it's for her constituents, too. Of course!

"I am working on their behalf, and they are seeing me work on their behalf," said Jackson Lee. "Many of them are moved by the moment."

Getting an aisle seat seems like it benefits Jackson Lee more than her constituents. I imagine that her constituents would rather have her spend the day working on their behalf rather than protecting her chosen seat. Taxpayers are paying her to work for them, not to get herself a few seconds on national television shaking the president's hand–although her policies are so bad for the American people, maybe we should be glad she doesn't spend more time trying to make them the law of the land.

The Oscars-like nature of the State of the Union doesn't end when the president leaves Congress. Following the State of the Union, the president sits down with journalists to discuss the speech. Adding to the silliness surrounding the event, in 2015 the president decided to sit down with three YouTube channel creators: Bethany Mota, GloZell Green, and Hank Green.

None of these YouTube stars had any experience in interviewing a politician–Bethany Mota is best known for putting together cute outfits, and GloZell's most popular videos are of her attempting to stick a condom up her nose and eating cinnamon–but that apparently doesn't matter. Obama was more than happy to sit there while the products and producers of YouTube culture asked him what superpower he would like to have, what his favorite television show is, and what career he wanted to have when he was a child.

In a super-surprising move, Hank asked about legalizing marijuana. After that, he asked the president to sign a picture of him with a receipt for a medication that he said he was able to get at a cheap price because of Obamacare. Hard-hitting journalism.

If you want to know what the state of our union is, there is no need to listen to the president's speech. Just look at the lack of seriousness surrounding the address. That is the state of our union.

Culture of Celebrity

Washington politicians are obsessed not only with building their own celebrity but also with being seen with celebrities. This is likely a by-product of wanting to have important friends in order to give the impression they themselves are important.

This culture is on full display at the annual White House Correspondents' Dinner. In the next chapter, we will see how the dinner reveals the overly (and overtly) cozy relationship between politicians and the press. Now let's take a look at what it reveals about how D.C. elites love to look at themselves in the mirror and get their pictures taken with famous people.

At the dinner, the elitist class, who are experts in social

climbing, turn into piranhas. They all fight to get selfies with the Hollywood actors in attendance. Why? So that they can tweet and Instagram it out for their colleagues to see.

Apparently, the behavior has become too much for many Hollywood actors. They have started to avoid the Beltway's most important social event. One Hollywood insider told the *Hollywood Reporter* back in 2014: "There are way too many A-listers who have had pretty weird experiences at the dinner. A lot of the people who have gone say they'll never do it again. The room is so crowded. It's uncontrolled. There's no limit to the number of people trying to get photos and autographs—and there's no way to hide from it. It's like the stars are animals in a cage. People go crazy when they see them. They act like a bunch of kids at the Kids' Choice Awards."

Others claim that the problem lies with Washington insiders' obsession with fame. "They're infatuated with anyone who is sort of famous," a previous attendee told the *Hollywood Reporter.* "People on reality TV shows are walking around like they're the secretary of state—and they're actually getting their pictures taken with the real secretary."

The Hollywood House

How do you know you're obsessed with celebrities? You start to confuse Hollywood actors with the characters they portray.

In 2012, Adam Lanza's horrific shooting spree at Sandy Hook Elementary School left twenty-seven victims dead, mostly children, and sparked a national conversation about mental health. Some time later, the White House decided to make Vice President Biden responsible for studying mental health and trying to understand its connection to violence.

Now, I know what you're thinking. The vice president is not the sanest member of the administration. Is he really the best person to study mental illness?

But putting aside the vice president's peculiarities, I thought enough of him that I figured he would at least go out and speak to experts and to Americans who have suffered with mental illness. Boy, was I wrong! In Washington, talking to experts in the field is a waste of time. Find a celebrity who plays one instead!

Biden asked actor Bradley Cooper to come to the White House to discuss mental health issues. Biden thought Cooper would have a lot to teach him because Cooper had starred in a film, *Silver Linings Playbook,* about a man who suffers from mental issues.

The meeting had many Americans scratching their heads, but in Washington the decision made complete sense. It was an opportunity for Biden to be seen with a celebrity, raise his profile, and cultivate a relationship with a movie star who may one day provide financial support to Biden if he chooses to run for office in the future. It was also a great opportunity to get a photo taken with a celebrity and tweet it out—which the vice president, of course, did.

This strange obsession with Hollywood doesn't just apply to the White House. It also extends to Capitol Hill.

In December 2012, the U.S. economy was still struggling to recover from the recession, and a severe threat loomed. On

January 1, 2013, the Bush tax cuts were set to expire. Military programs were going to be cut, and there would be about $500 billion in tax increases. Congress needed to come up with a deal before the January deadline in order to avoid the country falling off this "fiscal cliff."

You would think that Senate Majority Leader Harry Reid would be working around the clock in December to avoid going over the fiscal cliff, but that wasn't the case. Reid was busy playing event planner.

That's right—on December 19, 2012, just days away from the fiscal deadline, Reid adjourned the Senate so that our public servants could kick back, relax, and schmooze. He organized a special screening of the movie *Lincoln* and had Steven Spielberg and actor Daniel Day-Lewis join them.[9] That silly fiscal cliff wasn't on Reid's mind. What was on his mind was something entirely different—popcorn.

Reid was worried about the Congressional Auditorium's prohibition against food. No popcorn at the movie? That just wouldn't do! So Reid worked to get an exception from the Senate Rules Committee to serve movie snacks to the U.S. senators and their Hollywood guests.

A couple weeks after the screening—popcorn and all—Congress finally did strike a deal to avoid the fiscal cliff. It happened at two A.M. on January 1, 2013—just missing the deadline. Congress had paused for Hollywood stars and schmoozing. They had planned ahead to make sure the screening was a success. But when it comes to actually doing their job? They'll wait until the last minute—and then miss the deadline.

Cuomo's Death

Nothing highlights Washington's narcissism and obsession with status better than the reaction of its elites to the death of one of their own.

Take the death of former New York governor Mario Cuomo. When the news broke that he had passed away on January 1, 2015, did journalists and Washington insiders jump at the opportunity to commemorate him? No. But did they make sure that others in Washington knew how close they were with him? You bet.

For example, journalist Mike Barnicle was quick to publish a piece for the *Daily Beast* titled "Mario Cuomo Always Moving Us Toward the Light." But it would have been more appropriately titled "Let Me Explain to You How Much I Knew Mario Cuomo. You Should Be Impressed."

The piece starts off with Barnicle hanging out with Tim Russert (look at how important he is) and then describes a visit to a batting cage where he met Cuomo for the first time: "I still remember the first words I ever spoke to him too: 'Hey Governor, you're wearing cop's shoes,' as he stood there, a pair of black cordovans on his feet. I don't recall his reply but I do remember he laughed while he took a couple practice cuts, his thick hands gripping the bat lightly."

What? It's unclear how this tells us anything about Cuomo. But it doesn't matter, because it tells us that Barnicle knew Cuomo. And that's the main purpose of the piece, and most eulogies in D.C.

Barnicle then writes about the time he briefly visited

Cuomo's office with Tim Russert and their children. One of the kids had a ball in his hand, and Cuomo took it and tossed it back and forth with the eight-year-old. The kids had a gift for him, too, a T-shirt with "Baseball Spoken Here" stenciled across the front. And he had a gift for them: the lasting memory of time spent with a man who was bigger than the big dreams he had for those little children.

It's again unclear how this really tells us anything about Cuomo other than that Barnicle and his kids spent a brief moment with him. The piece makes it clear that Barnicle clearly didn't have a deep friendship or relationship with him, but he wanted so badly to make it seem that way. So he made sure to list every interaction they had ever had.

To add to the self-serving memorial, Barnicle, of course, included an unnecessary number of photos of his children in the piece. But that's how deaths in Washington, D.C., go. Pump out an essay about how you knew the person–even if you really didn't have much interaction with the deceased–in hopes that you will be considered part of the heritage of the person. In the rest of the country, a funeral is a time for loved ones to come together to bid farewell, but in Washington the death of a Washington insider is just another opportunity to show how important you are, to network with other Washington insiders, and to promote your individual brand.

The Death of a King

If you had driven past the Washington National Cathedral on October 29, 2014, you would have thought that a head of state had passed away. The streets were filled with satellite trucks, and cameras were perched on the lawn ready to film the mourners. Inside were the top Washingtonians in media and politics: Secretary of State John Kerry; NBC's Brian Williams and Tom Brokaw; Justice Stephen Breyer; PBS's Jim Lehrer; and mental health expert Joe Biden.

So, who was the dead head of state? None other than *Washington Post* executive editor Ben Bradlee. He had piloted the ship that symbolized, perhaps more than either political party, the D.C. establishment. He had been in the middle of the Watergate investigation. He had been at the *Post* for wars and impeachments. And he had seen the rise and near total collapse of print journalism.

Broadcast on C-SPAN for all the Washingtonians who couldn't fit into the cathedral, Bradlee's funeral was exactly what you would expect from D.C. People wanted to go to it not so much to pay their respects as to see and be seen. It was the must-go-to social event in town.

And the hottest ticket in town? The post-funeral reception. Only in Washington!

The reception was thrown by the best-known hostess in Washington—Bradlee's widow, Sally Quinn. As morbid as it sounds, an invitation to Quinn's Georgetown mansion on the day of her husband's funeral was widely considered an indication that you were someone.

The funeral reception felt like a typical Washington cocktail party. Numerous valet attendants were waiting outside as the A-list crowd arrived. After the guests had their cars valeted, a jazz band greeted them.

Inside, men in suits offered drinks to MSNBC's Chris Matthews and a cheerful Carl Bernstein of the *Washington Post.* Nancy Pelosi schmoozed with old friends. Amazon CEO Jeff Bezos laughed with a group of guests while the cameras flashed. The "mourners" sucked up and caught up and yukked it up.

Although the presence of professional photographers at a funeral party may seem bizarre, in Washington it's encouraged and appreciated. People want their photographs taken and posted in the paper later. Because, c'mon, they want their colleagues to know that they were important enough to get the invite.

Even the coverage after the party made it seem as though it were some red carpet event. Take, for example, the *Washington Post*'s write-up about the funeral reception. Describing the widow's attire, the *Post* reports, "She wore all black except for a vivid gold and enamel necklace and earring set—a family heirloom presented to George Crowninshield (Ben's great-great-great-grandfather) in 1815 by Pauline Bonaparte when he tried to save her brother from Elba, then was given to Sally by Ben."[10]

Having individuals with an exaggerated sense of entitlement in powerful positions is terrible because they're not interested in serving others; they're interested in serving themselves. Samuel Adams, one of our founding fathers, understood that electing virtuous people into office was central to making America succeed, because such people would lay the necessary groundwork for a prosperous and free nation. Adams realized, however, that "neither the wisest constitution nor the wisest laws will secure the liberty and happiness of a people whose manners are universally corrupt." He added that "the truest friend to the liberty of his country" is the person "who tries most to promote its virtue, and who . . . will not suffer a man to be chosen into any office of power and trust who is not a wise and virtuous man."[11]

Even though the founders made sure to create safeguards to protect the people from corruption, it's up to the American people to protect themselves from narcissistic men and women with low moral standards. Our founding fathers rightfully understood that narcissists in power become tone-deaf and are convinced they're deserving of whatever they can get their hands on. Their personal interests cloud their judgment, and their desires and needs take precedence over the needs of their constituents.

CHAPTER 7

Politicos and the Press:

A Love Story

The Club

It was a chilly night in November. The media and political elite were celebrating at the Hay-Adams—a small five-star luxury hotel in Washington, D.C. The cause of the celebration was Chris Matthews's latest book, *Jack Kennedy: Elusive Hero.*

My editor at the time, Tucker Carlson, asked me to stop by to see if I could snag some interviews with the guests. I wasn't on the guest list, but that didn't stop me from showing up. More surprisingly, it didn't stop the girl behind the lavish lobby's check-in table from letting me walk right into the main room ornately decorated with big fireplaces, regal fixtures, and rich, dark wood from wall to wall.

The room was flooded with a who's who of Washington. In just a single corner stood John Kerry, Alan Greenspan, and a slew of legislators, including Debbie Wasserman Schultz, Steny Hoyer, John Dingell Jr., Frank Lautenberg, Sheldon Whitehouse, and Claire McCaskill.

A host of journalists were laughing and schmoozing with the politicians. It was as if all of them were lifelong close friends. It seemed odd to me that these journalists were so friendly with the men and women whom they were paid to investigate and expose. But, of course, there a lot of things in Washington that seem odd to me.

The sad truth is that journalists and politicians are more like business partners than adversaries. That certainly appears to be the case for the reporters who were sipping cocktails and laughing it up at the shindig: NBC's Andrea Mitchell, Kelly O'Donnell, and Ken Strickland; the *Washington Post*'s Bob Woodward; *Time* magazine's Jay Newton-Small; CNN's Brianna Keilar; MSNBC's Joe Scarborough and president Phil Griffin; and the *Huffington Post*'s Howard Fineman.

The party was the embodiment of everything America hates about Washington: public servants sipping from martini glasses and snacking on pricey appetizers while schmoozing with the people who are supposed to be reporting on them.

This was nothing out of the ordinary, though. Every weekend in Washington, journalists and politicians have lunch with each other, drink with each other, and party with each other. Then, when Monday rolls around, the reporters don't ask the tough questions Americans want because they don't want to be mean to their buddies. Imagine how awkward it would be when they see them at the next cocktail party.

Washington journalists' desperate desire to be accepted as members of the politicians' exclusive club is great for the politicians. For a small price–giving the Washington press corps access to their lavish cocktail parties and their extravagant lives–they satisfy journalists' pathetic need for belonging. In exchange, the elected officials are given less scrutiny.

While at the party, I walked over to MSNBC's Chris Matthews, who was chatting with John Kerry. When the conversation appeared to end, I moved in.

"Hi, Mr. Matthews! My name is Michelle Fields. I'm a reporter for the *Daily Caller*. Can I ask you a few questions?"

"Sure!" said Matthews cheerfully.

As I began to ask him a question about the presidential field, he interrupted. "Wait, where are you from again?"

"The *Daily Caller.*"

"Ohhhhh!" said Matthews, rolling his eyes when he realized that I wasn't part of the media echo chamber. I wasn't part of the group of reporters who worship the ground he walks on. I'm not part of the circle of journalists who have to ask Matthews softball questions because I don't have to worry about a possible awkward encounter at next week's cocktail event.

"You can interview me," he said. "But only about my book. No other questions."

It's unlikely he would have set those same strict parameters for an interview with a reporter like, say, the *Huffington*

Post's Howard Fineman. But that's the difference. If you're not part of the club, they want you as far away from them as possible.

White House Correspondents' Dinner

The politicos who work at the White House know all about the importance of the club. They share with the media a strong bond and a complete lack of understanding about the problems facing Americans. And no event better illustrates the all-too-cozy relationship between our press corps and our elected officials than the annual White House Correspondents' Dinner.

Hosted by the White House Correspondents' Association and attended by the president and vice president, the White House Correspondents' Dinner is arguably the D.C. elites' most anticipated event of the year. From the first pre-party to the final hangover, Washington essentially stops. If Washington were a high school—and in many ways it is—this would be its prom. In fact, the event has now been dubbed "the nerd prom."

No matter how bad the economy is in America, each year more than 2,500 of the media elite gather in a Washington hotel ballroom and walk the red carpet in their expensive gowns and tuxedos. There are dozens of parties, dinners, after-parties, and post-hangover brunches—thrown by media giants such as Netflix, Google, the *Hill, Entertainment Tonight,* BuzzFeed, Facebook, Yahoo, and Tumblr. And every year, the spectacle gets bigger and bigger—more expensive and more expensive. For many Americans, struggling in this economy, there isn't all that much to celebrate. But in Washington, it's always considered appropriate to spend a small fortune so that the ruling class can celebrate itself.

Like the Chris Matthews book party, the White House Correspondents' Dinner shows what a corrupted relationship the D.C. press corps has with the people they purport to cover and hold accountable—though on a much larger scale. The same people who stand on the White House lawn and deliver information into Americans' living rooms spend all night drinking and partying with the officials they are supposed to be reporting on like a watchdog. The president and politicians get to fawn over reporters, and reporters fawn over the elected at an all-night circus that consists of getting drunk and introducing their significant others to government officials.

In 2015, Mark Leibovich, a strong critic of the White House Correspondents' Dinner, offered a special pre-party event. He decided to hold a media ethics colloquy at the Hilton Hotel—the venue of the WHCD—before the actual dinner.

How many journalists showed up to Leibovich's discussion? Zero. Instead, they walked the red carpet, took selfies, posted them to Instagram, and tweeted photos of themselves with the officials they are supposed to cover.

Reporter Patrick Gavin became so fed up with the White House Correspondents' Dinner that he decided to make a film about it. Gavin covered the WHCD for a decade for Politico. Every year he would attend the WHCD parties, after-parties, and brunches. But days before the 2014 WHCD Gavin left his job at Politico and decided to make the documentary *Nerd Prom* to provide an insider's look at what the event is really about.

Gavin tells me one of the most ridiculous parts of the dinner is "the way this town gets so giddy about it. . . . There is a level of electricity among the gang of five hundred that's unparalleled. There is a buzz under people's skin about it." The excitement has a lot to do with the fact that the event helps D.C. insiders evaluate their power. "It's a great way to assess your rank on the pecking order—depending on how many invites you get to the after-parties, you can then tell whether you're an A or a B on the social level." The event is "an annual gauge of your status."

He was also fed up that officials with a "ten percent approval rating, reporters included," would then throw a huge party to celebrate themselves: "We know everyone hates us and we don't give a shit. On top of that we flaunt it by throwing a super bowl for ourselves every year. That to me was obscene. . . . Representative government only thrives if it has the moral support of its people and we don't. . . . And on top of that we don't care."

King Obama

One of the issues the press ignores is President Obama's abuse of executive power. If you run a small business, pay an electric bill, or have health insurance, Obama's illegal abuse of his power has affected your life. And if you're like me, you probably want a press corps that scrutinizes the president's executive orders and reports on his lawlessness. But if you happened to see the 2015 White House Correspondents' Dinner, you know that that's not the kind of press corps we have.

At the 2015 dinner, President Obama addressed a room of A-list invitees and decided to make light of his excessive use of executive actions and memos.

During his address he declared: "This year I've promised to use more executive actions to get things done without Congress. My critics call this the imperial presidency. Truth is I just show up every day at my office and do my job. We've got a picture of this I think."

Reporters erupted into laughter as a photo went up on the screen of President Obama dressed as a king, sitting on the Iron Throne. Ironically, hanging in the background of the photo was a portrait of George Washington—the man who would not become king.

The Iron Throne comes from the TV series *Game of Thrones*. It's a throne built from the thousand swords surrendered by vanquished enemies. It's apparently hilarious when the president jokes about being king of his subjects and makes light of a topic—executive orders—that have angered the American people. The reporters in attendance laugh hysterically and take more sips from their champagne.

It's unclear what President Obama was thinking. Is he so out of touch with the concerns of the American people that he thinks it's funny to joke about his abuse of executive orders? Or is he finally just embracing what Washington has become—a royal court, with a king at the center of it?

Not Funny

In 2006, comedian Stephen Colbert was chosen to be the performer at the White House Correspondents' Dinner. He had just started his new show, *The Colbert Report,* and wasn't very well-known. But he was already adored by the D.C. elite, because his television personality was designed to mock Republicans and Fox News's Bill O'Reilly.

Based on Colbert's politics and popularity, you would expect him to be a hit when he performed at the White House Correspondents' Dinner. Not so much—because instead of pulling his punches like previous dinner performers and making a few good-natured jokes about the president and press corps, Colbert decided to eviscerate them.

Colbert began his routine by saying he had been asked to make an announcement: "Whoever parked fourteen black bulletproof SUVs out front, could you please move them? They are blocking in fourteen other black bulletproof SUVs, and they need to get out." Right off the bat, he was making fun of the D.C. elites' expensive penchant for their cherished chariots, and judging by the lack of laughter in the room, the D.C. elites were not amused.

After some jokes about President George W. Bush, Colbert turned his attention to the media: "Over the last five years you people were so good, over tax cuts, WMD intelligence, the effect of global warming. We Americans didn't want to know, and you had the courtesy not to try to find out. Those were good times, as far as we knew." Once again, many in the room were not amused.

Then, Colbert really went for the media's jugular: "But, listen, let's review the rules. Here's how it works: The president makes decisions. He's the Decider. The press secretary announces those decisions, and you people of the press type those decisions down. Make, announce, type. Just put 'em through a spell-check and go home. Get to know your family again. Make love to your wife. Write that novel you got kicking around in your head. You know, the one about the intrepid Washington reporter with the courage to stand up to the administration. You know—fiction!"

Many of the media sat there with stone faces. They hated the joke. They hated the whole routine. So did many of the public officials. The nearly twenty-minute-long performance by Colbert mocking the press corps, the president, and other politicos just did not sit well. For the first time in White House Correspondents' Dinner history, the political elite lost their sense of humor. In their eyes, Colbert had gone too far.

So, when it came time for these reporters to write about the White House Correspondents' Dinner, they decided to ignore it. They considered it uncomfortable, bad, even brutal—and thus unworthy of comment. For example, the *New York Times'* write-up of the event made almost no mention of the performance. And the few reporters who did decide to mention Colbert's performance panned it.

But then something happened that highlighted the great disconnect between America and the Beltway. The video of Colbert laying into the press corps and the government on national television was uploaded onto the Internet and went viral. The American public loved it!

Within forty-eight hours, Colbert's employer, Comedy Central, had received thousands of emails about the performance. The blogosphere couldn't stop raving about it. A website called ThankYouStephenColbert.org was temporarily set up out of appreciation. The performance had blown up on the Internet, much to the surprise and probably frustration of the press corps.

How did the press corps get the event so wrong in the stories? How did they not see the fact that Colbert was the star of the night?

After initially ignoring Colbert's performance, the *New York Times* ran a second write-up after the event. They felt the need to address Americans' outrage regarding the media's failure to give Colbert the attention he was due. But the *Times* story didn't touch on the reasons why the American people loved the performance so much–the fact that they were glad someone finally called out the press corps and the government! Instead, the article just laid out all of the criticisms of the performance.

The American people and the D.C. elite watched the same performance but walked away with diametrically opposed reactions–evidence that Washington is out of touch and unwilling to discuss the criticisms that many Americans have about them. Washington couldn't stand the fact that their favorite comedian came and made fun of their job performance and their culture right to their face. Americans, on the other hand, having lived and suffered because of the government's incompetence and the failure of the press corps to do its job, turned it into a national sensation.

JournoList

In 2008, Illinois senator Barack Obama was running for president. He built an impressive political operation, free of much of the drama that often plagues presidential campaigns. But in the spring of 2008, with Hillary Clinton still hanging on in the Democratic primaries, Obama's campaign was almost derailed because of videos that revealed his pastor, Jeremiah Wright, bashing America.

In one video, Wright said that, through the September 11 attacks, "America's chickens are coming home to roost." In another video, he said that the U.S. "government lied about inventing the HIV virus as a means of genocide against people of color." And in perhaps his most infamous video, Wright said: "The government gives [African Americans] the drugs, builds bigger prisons, passes a three-strike law and then wants us to sing 'God Bless America.' No, no, no, not God Bless America. God damn America—that's in the Bible—for killing innocent people. God damn America, for treating our citizens as less than human. God damn America, as long as she tries to act like she is God, and she is supreme."

In April 2008, during a presidential campaign debate, Senator Obama's close relationship with Wright was questioned—and for good reason. Here was a man who was trying to become the president of the United States, and he may have been heavily influenced by a pastor who was known for spewing hatred about whites, Jews, and the United States.

Did Obama agree with the opinions of his pastor? That's

what the American people wanted to know. So, during a debate moderated by Charles Gibson of ABC, Gibson asked Senator Obama about Jeremiah Wright: "Do you think Reverend Wright loves America as much as you do?"

It wasn't even a tough question, but it was enough to anger Gibson's colleagues. Although you would think that reporters would be interested in finding out more about Senator Obama's close relationship with this man who hated so much about America, Washington journalists thought Gibson was being too hard on the Democratic candidate. So they went to a Listserv called JournoList to express their anger.[1]

At the time, JournoList was filled with hundreds of political reporters, writers, and academics, including Nobel Prize-winning columnist Paul Krugman; policy wonks; bloggers such as Ezra Klein and Matthew Yglesias; and staffers from *Newsweek,* Politico, *Huffington Post,* the *New Republic,* the *Nation,* and the *New Yorker.*

One of the angry journalists on JournoList was Richard Kim of the *Nation.* Through the Listserv, he accused one of the moderators of the debate, George Stephanopoulos, of "being a disgusting little rat snake."[2]

Other writers on JournoList shared Kim's anger and discussed ways to take away the bad press from Obama regarding Rev. Jeremiah Wright. Spencer Ackerman from the *Washington Independent* suggested changing the subject by picking a conservative to accuse of racism: "Fred Barnes, Karl Rove, who cares–and call them racists."[3] Anything to help Obama.

Thomas Schaller from the *Baltimore Sun* sent a message titled "Why don't we use the power of this list to do something about the debate?" His idea was to put together a "smart statement expressing disgust" with the debate. "It would create quite a stir, I bet, and be a warning against future behavior of the sort."[4]

Michael Tomasky of the *Guardian* liked the idea of warning against bad behavior like asking legitimate questions about a liberal candidate's background and associations. "YES," he wrote. "A thousand times yes." Jared Bernstein, a writer who later went on to become chief economist for Vice President Biden, chimed in, saying he thought the letter ought to be "short, punchy and solely focused on vapidity of gotcha."[5]

In a matter of days, a letter signed by Washington journalists and analysts was delivered to ABC arguing that "the debate was a revolting descent into tabloid journalism and a gross disservice to Americans concerned about the great issues facing the nation and the world."[6]

JournoList, which is now defunct, successfully allowed journalists who wanted to collaborate to shield the government officials they liked best. But this isn't the only means by which reporters coordinate and protect the powerful–they also meet with them.

Meet the President

As if the media were not pro-Obama enough, President Obama strokes journalists' egos and cements their allegiance by inviting them to background briefings at the White

House. Guests agree not to reveal the officials who attend the meeting and not to quote anything that is said.

Typical meetings were held before and during the early implementation of Obamacare, which included the disastrous rollout of the president's healthcare website. The public was getting angrier and angrier about canceled health plans, rising premiums, and a website that wouldn't work.

So what was the White House to do? Call in reporters for an off-the-record, secretive briefing. At an early meeting, the White House hosted *Slate* blogger Matthew Yglesias, *American Prospect* staff writer Jamelle Bouie, and MSNBC's Benjy Sarlin.[7] All of them had written favorably about Obamacare and did so even after the rollout.

Then, when the Obamacare rollout did, in fact, end up being a disaster, the White House once again called in their troops: MSNBC's Lawrence O'Donnell, Ezra Klein, and Ed Schultz; Howard Fineman of the *Huffington Post;* David Corn of *Mother Jones;* and the *New Republic*'s Jonathan Krohn–a gathering with as much ideological diversity as a politburo meeting.[8]

These off-the-record meetings are indicative of how the media see themselves: as part of the establishment. The American people watching their televisions and turning to the pages of the news don't benefit from journalists attending an off-the-record meeting with the president, because the reporters can't reveal what they learned. The only people who gain something are the journalists, who earn power points among their peers because they were part of the crowd in the room.

Their relationship to the Obama administration is so close that some journalists are dreading the day that the president leaves the White House. And they have no problem admitting to it.

April Ryan is a case in point. A White House reporter for American Urban Radio Networks, she has covered the presidencies of Bill Clinton, George W. Bush, and Barack Obama. Her time covering President Obama has consisted of asking many, many softball questions at press briefings.

Like most of her colleagues, Ryan claims to be an objective reporter, even though she has a strong affection for the person she is supposed to be covering. In her book *The Presidency in Black and White,* Ryan talks about what it will be like for her, emotionally, when President Obama's second term in office is over. "I have got to now take in the moment because when he's gone, he's gone," says Ryan. "I will probably cry when he leaves, not because I like him or anything, and that's not even the case. I'm a reporter."[9]

You read that right. Ryan's a reporter who admits that she will shed tears when President Obama leaves the Oval Office. But in the same breath she claims she's objective. I guess when you define objectivity by the standards of the Washington press corps, you can be objective about the people you are enamored with.

Staffers-in-Waiting

To see just how incestuous the relationship is between reporters and the government, consider the case of Richard Stengel. In September 2013, Stengel was the top editor at *Time* magazine–but not for long. Stengel announced he was leaving *Time* for the State Department, where he was slated to be the under secretary for public diplomacy and public affairs. He was taking over the job of an old colleague, Tara Sonenshine, who had been a reporter for ABC News and *Newsweek* before working for Obama at Foggy Bottom.[10]

Stengel and Sonenshine were far from the first reporters to leave the world of journalism for the Obama administration. Stengel was joining a State Department that already included U.S. ambassador Samantha Power, who was formerly of *U.S. News & World Report.* On Stengel's staff at the State Department would be Desson Thomson, formerly of the *Washington Post.* Secretary of State John Kerry's office included Glen Johnson, formerly of the *Boston Globe,* and Douglas Frantz, formerly of the *New York Times.*

This is only a small example in an enormous government. The number of people who have decided to give up their press pass for a government job in the Obama administration is astounding. At least twenty-four former journalists work for Barack Obama.[11] This revolving door reflects the worldview of those in journalism. How can you be an objective reporter when your ideology is so aligned with those you are supposed to cover? How can the public be confident you aren't pulling your punches when you are reporting on a potential employer?

Even though the press was oftentimes ruthless in its criticism of our founding fathers, our forebears understood and appreciated the importance of a free press. Thomas Jefferson believed that a free press, which kept citizens informed, was essential to self-government. That's why he famously declared, "Were it left to me to decide whether we should have a government without newspapers, or newspapers without a government, I should not hesitate a moment to prefer the latter."[12]

Our press may be free to investigate and criticize the government, but its members are choosing not to do it. Jefferson didn't realize that the government and the press would one day work together. Journalists have become so aligned with political parties, candidates, politicians, and political issues that it's turned into one giant love affair that's threatening the livelihood of our democracy. The only way for this great American experiment to work is if the public is informed; it cannot succeed if the press won't print the truth out of fear of ruining a friendship or being passed up for a future position in government. This unhealthy relationship is depriving Americans of the information they need in order to make educated decisions.

Reporters were once watchdogs of the D.C. political class, bringing to light their corrupt ways, but today reporters are just working hard in hopes of joining them. Journalism is just a stepping-stone to a career in government. By constantly giving jobs to people in a struggling industry, the government is essentially telling journalists: "Don't mess with us. Don't get us upset. One day, your reporter gig may be up, and you're going to want a job with us." If only Obama were as good at creating jobs for the rest of the country.

CHAPTER 8

The American Family Business

Our founding fathers fought a war to rid themselves of a monarchy and sought to create a country where inherited power was illegal. To ensure that America didn't become a society with a nobility, the Constitution provides that "no Title of Nobility shall be granted by the United States." Unfortunately, that just isn't true anymore. We now live in a country where a recent commander in chief was the son of a previous president, and where at one point in the 2016 election cycle our two national parties were pushing to nominate the wife of an ex-president and the brother of an ex-president, who is also the son of an ex-president. Surrounding them are a band of elites who thrive by exchanging money and power for political favors.

Ask yourself this question: If John E. (Jeb) Bush were named Jeb Smith, would he have been a viable candidate for the presidency? Would his name be the talk of the chattering class? Would he have raised tens of millions of dollars at the drop of a hat?

While a famous surname can be used as a force for good to help those less fortunate, Jeb has done the opposite. He's used his surname, which is much like an enduring American franchise, to help himself and his friends become wealthier and more powerful, epitomizing the priorities, character, and cronyism that prevail in Washington. His rise from an up-and-coming political operator in Florida, to a governor, to a contender for the office of the presidency is an indication of what has become of American politics, where Washington is just one big playground for an elite governing class that cares only about its members and nothing about the American taxpayer.

A Bush Grows in Florida

When Jeb Bush's father was in power—first as vice president from 1981 to 1989, and then as president from 1989 to 1993—Jeb often took advantage of his father's powerful position to help his standing back in Florida. For example, when his father first became president, Jeb made sure that his father's staff knew they needed to make room in the president's schedule to help his son down in Florida. "I hope we can continue to get the president down to Miami as much as we used to when he was a mere VEEP," Jeb wrote.

Jeb relied on his family's place in high political office to grant favors on behalf of his allies. His requests were rarely about asking for help that would benefit ordinary American citizens. The requests Jeb made to his father's office and administration always seemed to have one thing in common: They would help someone in the Republican Party in Florida and, in turn, help Jeb.

In 1990, Jeb reached out to his father's office to set up a meeting with executives from Motorola, a major donor to the Republican Party in Florida. He wanted his dad to meet with Christopher Galvin, CEO of Motorola. "I urge you to visit with Motorola at your convenience," wrote Jeb, "to see first-hand how the Motorola experience can help our country (including agencies in the federal government)." He sent the message with an attachment containing a presentation from Motorola.

And just like that . . . voilà! President Bush and his chief of staff, John H. Sununu, ended up meeting with Motorola.

Jeb's efforts to set up the meeting proved beneficial to Galvin. When Jeb's brother George W. Bush became president, he appointed Galvin to a committee that advised the executive office on telecommunications issues.

The relationship has also been fruitful for Jeb Bush. When it became apparent that Jeb would be running for president of the United States in 2016, Galvin stepped in to help out. In February 2015, Galvin cochaired a fancy soiree at the Fairmont Chicago Millennium Park hotel. It was a fundraiser for Jeb where he delivered his first major foreign policy speech. At the event, Jeb sat at the main table with some of the biggest names in business, including the man whom Jeb had helped many years before–former Motorola CEO Christopher Galvin.

To be sure, there would have been nothing wrong with Jeb using his connections to his father's White House in an effort to help the Florida public at large. But that's not what Jeb was doing. His communications don't show a desire to ask his dad for help in promoting policy programs that would benefit ordinary citizens. Instead, they show a man who was determined to help his cronies, who would then be willing to help him later.

The meeting Jeb arranged for Motorola was far from an exception. It was the norm. In fact, he apparently pinged the White House so much that his father's staff members had to come up with new ways to deal with the influx of his requests. One solution, proposed by an assistant to his father named Jane Kenny, was for Jeb to stop sending requests directly to government agencies and offices. She politely asked him to just send all requests to her. "That way," Kenny wrote, "there will be no chance for misunderstanding."

Dear Dad: Please Make My Friend U.S. Attorney

Jeb's efforts started as early as 1989, when there was a vacancy for the position of U.S. attorney for the Southern District of Florida. Jeb had a friend, Dexter Lehtinen, who was a close political ally of his. Lehtinen didn't have the experience for the job and was disliked by many who worked with him. But Jeb was so determined to help out Lehtinen that not only did he call up his father's chief of staff, Craig Fuller, but he also sent him a handwritten note giving his recommendation for Lehtinen.

It's hard to imagine any state politician having the guts to ask the vice president of the United States to nominate someone as a U.S. attorney. But when you're part of an American dynasty, that's just how things go.

Fuller took the request of his boss's son seriously. He sent a note to the assistant to the vice president, Thomas Collamore. The note included Lehtinen's résumé and informed Collamore that "Jeb thinks [he] would be a good candidate in South Florida."

President Reagan appointed Lehtinen to an interim position, but Jeb was unhappy with that position for his ally. So when Jeb's father finally became president, Jeb decided to push for Lehtinen to get confirmed by the U.S. Senate. He sent a note to his father's counsel, C. Boyden Gray, letting him know that he was upset that Lehtinen's name had not gone to the Senate for confirmation.

Meanwhile, the press was turning out story after story that raised many red flags. First off, critics in the press accused Lehtinen of lacking experience and having an explosive temper.[1] Then Lehtinen's girlfriend and ex-wife came forward and alleged that Lehtinen had verbally and physically abused them.[2] There were also former coworkers of his who detailed his explosive temper and tendency to get violent.[3] Despite all of these red flags, Jeb was determined to get Lehtinen the position. Keep in mind–this isn't just any position–this is U.S. attorney. This is a position that influences decisions dealing with crime and fairness in America. You would think having someone with an alleged bad temper and history of domestic abuse would be a terrible candidate. But not in Jeb's mind. He knew of the allegations but still pushed for him.

Jeb acknowledged in his letter to C. Boyden Gray that Lehtinen had character flaws, stating that "despite Dexter's human frailties . . . he is being treated unfairly by the press."

And he had a stern message for the president's counsel: "Boyden. It is time to act."

The Senate never ended up confirming Lehtinen. In fact, they rebuffed him for the post, not once, but twice. Despite the Senate's snubs, Lehtinen served as interim U.S. attorney in south Florida for three years. He was a controversial figure with a worrisome background who shouldn't have ever been considered for the position. But Jeb helped make it happen. Not surprisingly, during Lehtinen's tenure there were complaints from his staff about his volatile personality.

Lehtinen's story ends exactly how you'd imagine it: The Justice Department opened an inquiry into Lehtinen after allegations of misconduct were made against him. Lehtinen abruptly resigned. The day that he resigned, about forty prosecutors went to a local bar near the federal courthouse to celebrate his resignation.[4] According to reports, they drank alcohol, hugged one another, and played James Brown's "I Feel Good" on repeat.[5] The only people who were unhappy about the resignation: Dexter Lehtinen and Jeb Bush.

The request shows Jeb's penchant for cronyism, because Lehtinen was an old friend. Jeb had been the manager of the congressional campaign of Lehtinen's wife, Ileana Ros-

Lehtinen. The recommendation is just another example of how Jeb operates. He isn't interested in policy changes that help the average American who is suffering. Instead, he uses his connections to help those who are already powerful become more powerful.

Jeb continued that modus operandi when it came time for a U.S. Supreme Court appointment. Once again, he lobbied his father on behalf of one of his allies in south Florida. Jeb suggested Peter T. Fay, a federal appellate judge from Miami. He sent another note to the White House counsel, C. Boyden Gray, with his recommendation for Fay and attached Fay's résumé.

Gray responded by informing Jeb that his ally would get "thoughtful consideration." Jeb recommended other friends for the head of White House security and the IRS commissioner.

The notion that a state politician would have a say in the appointment of a Supreme Court justice is baffling. Jeb's pattern of behavior shows an outrageous sense of entitlement, which is the most worrying aspect of having children of political dynasties run the country. Evidence of this sense of entitlement can be seen in the notes from Jeb to the White House. He didn't want to earn his way to the top through hard work. Instead, he wanted to exchange political favors and cash in on family ties.

One can argue that using your connections in Washington isn't anything new. After all, most people use their networks to further themselves. But the problem with sons or daughters of a political dynasty who are fortunate enough to be given a seat at the political table is that they can't understand the struggles of the American people. They've spent their careers pretty much always getting what they want. They never struggle. They never fail. They didn't have to fight for that seat at the table. They were given that seat and, if they didn't get it, they could just shoot an email to Dad asking for one. How can they truly understand how average Americans think, want, and need, if they've never had to deal with so many of the problems that regular folks go through? The type of life and upbringing that a member of a political dynasty has is anything but representative of the experience of the average American. So what makes them think that they are best fit to represent them?

Another consequence of these American dynasties is that political power becomes concentrated in the hands of one family and their friends. Dynasties are in the business of back-scratching and exchanging favors, which seems to be Jeb's specialty. He wasn't even in the Bush administration, yet he was pressuring his father and his father's staff to nominate his friends.

Jeb has had two family members who have served in the White House. Throughout his campaign, he carried with him the baggage of family political debts and favors that need to be fulfilled, as is the case with so many of our government officials.

Moreover, if you have the same family and their allies in the White House over and over again, how do new, fresh ideas come about? A Jeb presidency likely would have been one in which cabinet positions were filled with people who, at one point, helped out or worked for the Bush dynasty.

This pushes out prospective people who may have better and newer ideas for America.

This is exactly why our forefathers warned us of dynasties. Our government's legitimacy is negatively impacted when a small number of families and their allies occupy the highest office in America. And what does it say about our government that, as soon as a political elite like George H. W. Bush has a child, the child is groomed for dynastic succession? It compromises our democracy, fosters cronyism, and weakens the quality of representation.

We like to tell our children that they can grow up to be president if they work hard and really want it. But the reality is that Americans under the age of fifty-seven have only been able to vote in one presidential election cycle, the 2012 election, that didn't have someone in the Bush or Clinton family on the ballot in the general election or a primary. Not only is this demoralizing for Americans, especially young ones, but it also ruins our image as the country of opportunity. How can we seriously tell younger generations that we are the land of opportunity when the same two families, and their allies, seem to control much of Washington? The sad truth is that politics in America is no longer about serving the community; it's about getting into the family business and serving your friends.

Banking on a Last Name

In comic books, Spider-Man's Uncle Ben tells his nephew that with great power comes great responsibility. But when it comes to American political dynasties, dads might as well tell their children that with power comes money. A lot of money.

With a last name like Bush, Jeb knew he could make millions very easily, and when he left political office in 2007 he had one goal: build up his wealth by cashing in on his surname. At the time, his net worth was $1.3 million. For an average American, that is quite a fortune, but for Jeb it was nothing. He wanted more money, so he used his last name to enrich himself.

Jeb went about his quest for money by looking for the companies that were willing to give him the biggest paycheck. And, not surprisingly, Jeb regularly found himself associating with shady businesses and becoming entangled in high-profile business disasters.

Jeb seemed to care little about the values or purpose of the business, so long as it generated money for him. His business background shows a man with poor judgment and a man motivated by greed.

Jeb's Trifecta of Failure: InnoVida, Lehman Brothers, and Swisher Hygiene

In 2007, InnoVida was a Miami start-up that manufactured building materials. The flashy, jet-setting Venezuelan entrepreneur Claudio Osorio created the company. He was a prominent donor for the Democratic Party. Osorio and his wife were once considered a power couple and held political fundraisers at their $14.9 million waterfront property in

Miami. They would often host events attended by Bill Clinton, Barack Obama, Hillary Clinton, and other Democratic politicians.

At the time, Jeb Bush wanted money, a lot of money. He had just left the governor's mansion and was approached by Osorio with the opportunity to become a paid consultant for InnoVida. Osorio needed to raise funds, and he figured that with a member of the Bush dynasty on staff, investors would be willing to come on board.

The business relationship ended up becoming a perfect match. Jeb brought credibility to the company, and the company brought him tremendous wealth. In 2007, Jeb signed on the dotted line and became a consultant, raking in $15,000 a month. Less than a year later, he received 250,000 stock options. But then things got messy.

In 2010, Haiti was hit with an earthquake, and the U.S. government's Overseas Private Investment Corporation (OPIC) gave InnoVida a $10 million loan to help rebuild some of the damaged areas. OPIC documents declared, "This project will provide immediate affordable pre-fabricated housing opportunities for [Haiti's] displaced individuals. In addition, the project's sponsor will construct a housing manufacturing facility that will produce disaster[-] and pest-resistant, energy-efficient and sustainable housing and building solutions. The project's housing construction and manufacturing activities will result in 37 new jobs for Haitians, who will receive both in-country and foreign training for ongoing operations."

Sounds like a great project, right? The only problem was

that the money from Jeb and Osorio's company never went to Haitians. According to the FBI, while many Haitians were living in tents and waiting for these homes to be built, Osorio used the government money "to repay investors and for his and his co-conspirators' personal benefit and to further the fraud scheme." The company eventually went bankrupt, and Osorio was indicted. He ended up admitting that he had scammed investors out of $40 million and had also ripped off the U.S. government.

The problem for Jeb Bush is not that he was involved in the fraud scheme (he wasn't) or that he had knowledge of what was going on (he didn't). The problem is that Bush sold his name to a corrupt company in order to give the company, in Osorio's words, "an air of legitimacy."

The real question for Bush is why he was willing to lend Osorio "an air of legitimacy" even though Osorio had been involved in financial irregularities before then. Prior to Bush signing up for InnoVida, Osorio had been in trouble for lying about the financial soundness of his previous company, CHS Electronics. The story of the rise and fall of CHS Electronics is similar to the story of InnoVida. The company had at one point been a *Fortune* 500 company, but then evidence of false financial documents regarding the health of the company and irregular accounting documents emerged. CHS Electronics ended up filing for bankruptcy and settled a securities fraud class action lawsuit with its shareholders.

An aide to Bush told the *New York Times* that he had diligently looked into InnoVida before joining the company. The aide claims Bush ran a background check on Osorio. However, if Bush had done a thorough background check, Osorio's previous case would have undoubtedly appeared. There is no way a background search wouldn't have uncovered a paper trail that detailed how Osorio had forged documents and propped up a financially unhealthy business that eventually went bankrupt. Either Jeb saw it and chose to ignore it because of his overwhelming desire to become wealthy, or he has the investigating talents of Mr. Magoo.

Jeb has a habit of associating himself with companies that are either on the verge of collapse or in the midst of doing something unethical and illegal. Take, for example, the former banking giant Lehman Brothers. Jeb was brought on as a consultant because of his last name and connections. During the financial crisis, Lehman called on Jeb to meet with Mexican billionaire Carlos Slim. Unfortunately for Jeb, the effort proved unsuccessful. Lehman Brothers ended up filing for bankruptcy, which helped take down the American economy and cost American taxpayers billions of dollars.

Jeb's relationship with Swisher Hygiene is another dent in his business portfolio. While he was sitting on the soap maker's board of directors and receiving more than $300,000 in stocks and cash, the company was issuing shady financial statements and concealing its true financial situation. Swisher Hygiene executives told the *New York Times* that during Bush's time with the company "their financial statements were unreliable and their accounting practices inadequate." In the end, once again, there was a class action lawsuit. The case included Jeb, and accused him and the board of "permitting the company to disseminate material misrepresentations and omissions to the investing public and abdicating his or her oversight responsibilities to the Company." The lawsuit ended with a settlement.

Jeb's Fugitive Friend

Jeb Bush's determination to capitalize on his name and gain wealth has thrown him into a number of other questionable situations. In 1985, he worked for a man named Miguel Recarey, who paid him $75,000 for real estate consulting. Jeb's job was to find Recarey a property for his company, but he never actually finalized any real estate purchase for Recarey or his company.

Who is Recarey, you may ask?

Recarey is a felon who had ties to organized crime in Miami. After he didn't file income taxes in 1969 and 1970, he went to prison for tax evasion. But despite all the red flags, Jeb chose to lobby his father's administration on behalf of Recarey.

In 1992, when Jeb's father was president, Jeb reached out to the Department of Health and Human Services to ask for a favor on behalf of Miguel Recarey. At the time, Recarey was CEO of International Medical Centers, and he had a pending application for the renewal of a waiver that would have allowed Recarey's company to receive more than half of its revenue from Medicare reimbursements. What Jeb (presumably) didn't know is that Recarey needed this waiver in order to commit his scheme of stealing money from Medicare.

Former HHS secretary Margaret Heckler claims that Jeb

called her personally on behalf of Recarey. Heckler took the request seriously because of her belief, and the belief of those in political establishment, that Jeb was the heir to the presidency. "Jeb was one that I and friends of the Bushes always thought would be president," she said.

Heckler's chief of staff, C. McClain Haddow, speaking before the House Government Operations subcommittee about Jeb's request, said, "Ms. Heckler's description of it and the reason why she thought it was important I thought were blatantly political. She was just very interested in maintaining a close personal relationship with Mr. Bush, because she perceived there was a political future for her in doing so."

In the end, IMC collected up to $1 billion from Medicare. Meanwhile, the embezzling Recarey overcharged Medicare. The scheme eventually was revealed, but Recarey never ended up spending time in prison. He first fled to Venezuela and now lives as a wealthy fugitive in Spain.

The Revolving Door

Jeb's association with Miguel Recarey is just another example of what appears to be a willingness to associate with unethical individuals in order to make money. It also shows what the typical postpolitical career looks like: lucrative gigs on the boards of companies that pay exorbitant amounts of money to former politicians because they want access to the networks of politicians who are willing to cash in on their public work at the expense of the American taxpayer.

Here's what usually happens. The former politicians get

paid to ask the government for favors. Then, the former politicians call up their buddies in the government and get a meeting, or a waiver, or some other kind of special treatment. It allows for personal relationships, rather than what's good for the American people, to drive the policy decisions in Washington.

When you've got politicians making decisions based on a political favor they owe to a former colleague, it's a threat to our democracy. Decisions should be based on what's best for the American people and not on whether a public servant is personally indebted to someone. It distorts the policy-making process, erodes trust among the American people, and turns our republic into a game rigged in favor of the elite and well connected. Our founders believed that republics rot from within, and decay typically begins at the top. They observed that unscrupulous behavior from top officials ends up making its way down to the rest of society and threatening the entire country. That's why elected officials are expected to conduct themselves with the highest scruples and make whatever sacrifices are necessary for the sake of transparency and integrity. Allowing our officials to govern through favors undermines our democratic process and sets America up to become like the corrupt European-style governments that our founding fathers detested.

Jeb Bush embraced this revolving door with enthusiasm— and success. In his case, he could call up someone he wanted to ask for a favor, and the person would often feel obligated to do it because of Jeb's family's influence.

In the past ten years, Jeb has gone from the public sector to the private sector, and now he wants to go back to the public sector. How do we know that, if he had made it to the White House, he wouldn't have shown favoritism to the private industries, companies, and bosses that paid him tons of money to do their bidding for the past eight years?

Several of those bosses were far from ethical. But not only was Bush willing to associate with sketchy characters; he was also willing to work with groups that are diametrically opposed to what he purports to believe in. He appears to be willing to sacrifice his political beliefs and lend his name to any group, so long as the price is right.

For example, Jeb, like most of his Republican colleagues, has been vocal about his opposition to Obamacare, calling it "flawed to the core" and saying that it "doesn't work." However, since 2007, Jeb has earned more than $2 million for being a board member of hospital owner Tenet Healthcare, which has been a huge supporter of Obamacare.

Tenet has been an aggressive force when it comes to getting Americans signed up for Obamacare. It has also not been shy about discussing how happy it is with Obamacare and the boon it has provided for the company. So while Bush was publicly opposing Obamacare, he was privately cashing in on it.

Tenet Healthcare has also been known to engage in some unethical business practices. It has been accused of overbilling Medicare. In 2012, Tenet settled with the U.S. Justice Department and agreed to pay $42.75 million for violating the False Claims Act.

How many questionable business associations does that

make for Jeb Bush? So many that I've stopped keeping count. Like others in Washington, Jeb wants to serve himself, and not his country. Why else would he take money from so many companies that have a history of defrauding investors and the American taxpayer?

China and 2016

Jeb's most profitable and important business ally is one of America's biggest rivals: China. Jeb has a long history of doing business with China and opening doors for the Chinese, and this cozy relationship is a serious problem.

Before Jeb's run for office in 2016, many in the political world had called him "the heir" to the presidency. Therefore, in the eyes of the Chinese, Jeb wasn't your regular politician. He was pretty much the president-in-waiting, and the Chinese were preparing to cash in on the next Bush presidency.

When Jeb arrived in Hainan, China, in 2011 to improve relations between Chinese and Florida businesses, he received the type of greeting that an ambassador or president of the United States would have received. The governor of Hainan—who had visited Florida earlier in the year—greeted Bush with a necklace of flowers.

This close relationship with China and the Chinese province of Hainan has proven to be fruitful for Jeb. With the backing of a Chinese conglomerate, Bush set up an offshore private equity fund called BH Logistics. He called on his contacts in Hainan, and he was able to raise over $25 million for his funds, thanks to investors like the Hainan-based HNA Group.

Jeb also helped run another fund called BH Global Aviation. According to SEC filings in 2014, 98 percent of its funding comes from foreign citizens. The structure of the fund has been set up so that the investors are anonymous. However, one of the names of the investors has been disclosed: Guang Yang. He is the CEO of a Beijing company called Finergy Capital, and, not surprisingly, he has ties to Hainan. In 2010 Yang partnered with Hainan Airlines and bought an upscale country club in California.

Because of the lack of transparency with Jeb's funds, one cannot fully know the nature of his investors and investments. However, according to sources close to Jeb, BH Global Aviation has invested in a Hong Kong company called Hawker Pacific.

Jeb's close economic ties to China raise the question: How do the American people know that these wealthy and powerful Chinese citizens didn't build a relationship and invest in Jeb's funds in an attempt to make him beholden to China? How do we know they didn't give money in order to buy influence from the man they considered the "heir to the presidency"?

It's questionable whether politicians can ever truly be independent when they have a history of being in bed with the elite and powerful of China. After all, the reason why many outside investors are willing to give money to former politicians is because they hope they can influence them. When politicians like Jeb speak about foreign policy, specifically about China, can he truly be independent, considering his long, complex, and lucrative relationship with the nation's powerful elite? It certainly looks like a clear conflict of interest for a man who wanted to become our nation's commander in chief.

Granted, this isn't something unique. Another presidential candidate is also in bed with foreign countries: Hillary Clinton.

Another Dynasty, the Same Old Story

In March 2015, Hillary Clinton scheduled a number of high-profile speaking engagements focused on women's rights. She wanted to commemorate the memorable 1995 speech she gave on women's rights in Beijing. During the 1995 speech, the then first lady said that "human rights are women's rights, and women's rights are human rights."

Hillary's March 2015 speaking engagements were also an opportunity to reintroduce her to the American voters in the run-up to the 2016 election. The carefully planned events were meant to remind voters that, when it comes to empowering women, Hillary is at the forefront.

But the truth is that Hillary is really interested in helping only one woman: herself. Hillary speaks about how important women's rights are, yet she is willing to take money from Saudi Arabia, whose government treats women terribly. Saudi Arabia has given more than $10 million to the Clinton Foundation.

Hillary had the opportunity to publicly turn down the

donation from Saudi Arabia and blast its shameful record on women's rights. That would have been a strong statement against a government that is actually waging a war on women (rather than the fake war on women Democrats invented a few years ago). But unfortunately Hillary talks a big game about being a champion for women, but when a check comes in from a kingdom that is responsible for violence against women, she has no problem cashing it.

In 2010, the country of Algeria spent hundreds of thousands of dollars lobbying Hillary's State Department on human rights issues. At the same time, the Embassy of Algeria, coincidentally, decided to make a first-time unsolicited donation to Hillary's foundation. Similarly, the United Arab Emirates gave between $1 million and $5 million to the foundation, while Germany gave between $100,000 and $250,000.

Most of these donations from foreign governments were legal because of an ethics agreement that Hillary signed when she became secretary of state. The agreement said she had to seek approval from the State Department before accepting foreign donations from any country that was not already an existing donor to Clinton's foundation. But any increase in donations and any donation from a new country had to be approved by the State Department's ethics department.

Hillary, however, violated the agreement. The Clinton Foundation accepted money from a new donor, Algeria, without seeking approval from the State Department. In fact, the Clinton Foundation never sent any donations over to the State Department to review. When you're a Clinton, you don't have to follow the rules.

Algeria is the only country that actually violated the requirements for disclosure per the agreement. But the fact that a secretary of state's family foundation was collecting donations from foreign governments was unsavory to say the least. You had a foreign nation funneling money to the sitting secretary of state (and a potential future president) through her foundation.

Why were the Saudis and other governments giving millions of dollars to the Clinton Foundation? Are the Saudis just that nice? So nice that they will throw millions of dollars at the Clinton Foundation, even while they refuse to help the women of their own country? Or were they buying influence in the Obama administration and investing in a future Hillary Clinton presidency?

These countries' leaders aren't stupid. They knew of Hillary's presidential ambitions, and they understood the scope of her influence in Washington. The countries that gave money to the foundation include Algeria, the Dominican Republic, Kuwait, Oman, and Qatar, which was spending millions of dollars on lobbyists in Washington.

Many Clinton defenders note that there is no smoking gun—no evidence of a quid pro quo. So, all is okay, right? Our founding fathers would disagree. They believed in corruption in a broader sense, meaning there didn't need to be an actual exchange of cash for them to view a transaction between government officials as corruption. They believed that any gift from a foreign government to an American official, even if there isn't evidence of a quid pro quo, was a threat to the republic. They believed that the appearance of corruption was dangerous to America because the appearance of corruption could lead to actual corruption by clouding the judgment of the government official who received the gift. The idea to include the Emoluments Clause, which forbids the acceptance of gifts from foreign governments without congressional approval, in our Constitution arose from a gift that Benjamin Franklin received from King Louis XVI. When Benjamin Franklin was U.S. ambassador to France, the king gave Franklin a diamond-encrusted box with the king's portrait on it. At the time, it was common for kings to give gifts to foreign officials and wasn't viewed as controversial in Europe.

Franklin didn't offer him anything in return for the lavish gift, but our founders in America were concerned. To them, this was corruption. They were concerned that Franklin might be more sympathetic (either intentionally or unintentionally) toward the king in his future dealings because of the kind gesture. George Mason worried about the impact of foreign gifts, and argued during the Constitutional Convention: "If we do not provide against corruption, our government will soon be at an end." If our founders were here to witness the dealings of Clinton and foreign governments, they would be appalled.

But the Clinton Foundation says that it's not a big deal because the money that it receives from foreign governments goes toward helping the world. Turns out, that's not exactly true. Between 2009 and 2012, the Clinton Foundation raised over $500 million, yet only 15 percent of that money went toward program grants.[6]

The Clinton Foundation operates as one big piggy bank for Hillary and her family. It provides luxurious accommodations for her family, and it gives her a way to meet mega-rich donors. From 2009 to 2012, the foundation spent a whopping $25 million on lavish travel expenses for the Clintons.[7] In 2013 alone, the foundation spent more than $8 million on travel expenses for Hillary, Bill, and Chelsea. The rest of its money goes toward salaries and "other expenses." The foundation doesn't detail in its tax forms what those "other expenses" are, but they're not going to programs to save the world. It's no surprise that Charity Navigator, an independent group that rates charities and helps donors navigate the charity-giving process, put the Clinton Foundation on the "watch list." The list is intended to warn donors of nonprofits that are troublesome.

All in the Family

What happens if Hillary Clinton becomes president and has to deal with a foreign country that gave her money? Will she rise above it? Or will she be like everyone else in Washington—a town that is all about exchanging political favors? How do the American people know that, if a Clinton was to get back into the White House, the president wouldn't have loyalty to these countries and individuals?

In 2008, Hillary talked about the three A.M. phone call that a president might get. Fair enough. Imagine this call.

The phone rings in the White House. A wealthy donor or investor is on the line. He's from another country. President Hillary Clinton picks up the phone. Can the American people have faith that she will have the interests of the United States in mind? Would we feel any more confident if President Jeb Bush were answering the call?

These two families are the leading royal families in America. They help out their aristocratic friends and continue to work to make sure that other family members rise in power. When I spoke to Doug Wead, who served as special assistant and spiritual adviser for President George H. W. Bush, he told me that the Bush families are acutely aware that they're functioning like a royal family. Wead tells me that the Bushes, "have always been very conscious and sensitive to this whole idea of the dynasty. . . . In fact I've heard Herbert Walker say 'Don't use that word.'" He adds that President H. W. Bush "gets irritated when someone uses that word [and] they've sent a signal to their staff that nobody says that word."

However, before Jeb Bush announced that he would run for president, former first lady Barbara Bush was asked whether she would like to see her son Jeb run for office. She replied, "No, I really don't. I think it's a great country. There are a lot of great families. There are other people out there that are very qualified, and we've had enough Bushes." The clip went viral because Americans found it refreshing to hear someone in the Bush clan admit what so many of us think, which is that we're tired of the Bush and Clinton families.

However, Wead says the entire quote was less than genuine and was a calculated attempt to get in front of the subject before it became an issue.

"She said it because she's a very good politician. Very smart," he tells me. The first lady eventually reversed course and began helping Jeb raise money. In a letter Barbara Bush sent to donors in spring 2015, she claimed that her son would be great for office because "our problems are so profound that America needs a leader who can renew the promise of this great nation." According to her, that means having a leader with the last name Bush. Wead tells me that the Bush family saw the Jeb Bush presidential run as a win-win situation and an opportunity to "reset the image" of the Bush family, which was tarnished by George W. Bush's presidency. Best-case scenario for the Bush family: Another Bush gets the White House. Worst-case scenario: Jeb runs, "gets in the debates, handles himself with dignity, and passes on the torch to [his son] George P.," says Wead. All in all, a good outcome for America's aristocracy.

The Clintons and the Bushes are more alike than different. Dynasties like theirs are what our founding fathers fought against when they revolted from King George. And whether or not you think that the previous Bush and Clinton administrations were good for the nation, there is something fundamentally un-American about the idea that we are going to elect King Clinton's queen or another one of King George's progeny.

CHAPTER 9

All the President's Money Men:

Or, How to Be an Ambassador Without Really Trying

I n the early years of the Roman Empire, an emperor named Caligula ruled with a style of reckless cruelty that might give even Joffrey Baratheon pause. Like the teenage tyrant on *Game of Thrones,* Caligula ordered the execution of innocents for his own amusement. On one occasion, he allegedly fed a section of an audience to the lions to relieve his boredom. He also caused mass starvation through his wasteful spending on a bridge to honor his own divinity, and having played suitor and pimp to his own sisters, he displayed a sexual appetite beyond even Clintonesque proportions.

There was, however, someone besides himself for whom Caligula did seem to have a genuine concern, someone he doted on, someone whose care he made the highest of priorities. This certain someone was Incitatus—his horse. The emperor adored his horse so much that, according to legend, he even appointed Incitatus to the Roman Senate.

Nearly 1,800 years later, America's founding fathers were all too familiar with the tale of Caligula's preposterous appointment, as well as the world's long history of incompetent tyrants making incompetent appointments. For millennia, absolute power had been exercised not just by dictators from their thrones, but by dictators through their minions, ministers, and satraps. Part of the genius of our Constitution's framers was to insist on the separation of powers, and a system of checks and balances in which presidential appointments would face the scrutiny of the Senate's "advice and consent." Article II of the Constitution says that only with the Senate's "advice and consent" can the president "appoint Ambassadors, other public Ministers and Consuls, Judges of the supreme Court, and all other Officers of the United States."

Contrary to the manner in which the Senate in recent decades has abused its power and blocked qualified appointees such as Robert Bork and John Bolton simply because liberals didn't agree with them, the founders expected the Senate to serve as a check primarily on cronyism and nepotism. To be sure, it wasn't likely any president would be so bold as to appoint his horse to an official position, but they couldn't be sure that a future president would refrain from nominating unqualified appointees as a payback for political favors.

The framers' intent was made clear in the Federalist Papers, where Alexander Hamilton wrote that the Senate's "advice and consent" power "would be an excellent check upon a spirit of favoritism in the President, and would tend greatly to prevent the appointment of unfit characters," including those picked only because of "family connection" and "personal attachment."

Unfortunately, the establishment in Washington, D.C., has turned this paradigm on its head–especially when it comes to the first kind of offices listed by the Constitution when requiring "advice and consent": ambassadors. Today, not only are ambassadors picked because of their personal connection to the president; for many embassy posts, it is impossible to be picked unless you have a personal connection, which almost always includes a record of raising money for the president's political party.

In the Footsteps of Adams, Jefferson, and Franklin

Do you want to live in a beautiful mansion in Rome, Paris, or London, surrounded by sprawling grounds and beautiful artwork? Be an ambassador! Do you have a complete lack of experience as a diplomat? No worries! Competence and skill are optional. All you have to do is give the president's political party a lot of money!

Yes, for the right price you can join the ranks of John Adams and John Quincy Adams and become U.S. ambassador to the United Kingdom! Not only do you get an awesome job title and international bragging rights, but you can also live in one of the grandest mansions in all of London, the Winfield House. With twelve acres of land, it is the second largest private garden in London (right behind Buckingham Palace).[1] And wait until you see the inside! It's filled with lovely porcelain, beautiful chandeliers, priceless antiques, and beautiful art. Queen Elizabeth I used it for entertaining dignitaries, and now you can live in it with the title of ambassador!

Or maybe Rome is more up your alley?

For the right price you can live in the Villa Taverna, where the U.S. ambassador to Italy resides. You get to go down in history with the likes of former ambassador Clare Boothe Luce. And if you're a wine lover, oh boy, are you in luck! Your residence includes a $1 million wine cellar with five thousand bottles. The Taverna features thirty-five rooms, sprawling gardens, antiques, and priceless art, such as three-hundred-year-old busts of Roman emperors.[2]

But maybe you prefer fresh baguettes, chic fashion, and a title once carried by the likes of Benjamin Franklin, James Monroe, and Thomas Jefferson? Then U.S. ambassador to France is probably more your scene. Granted, Franklin, Monroe, and Jefferson were pretty qualified for their jobs, but that was back then! Those suckers needed to have an impressive résumé, but not today. For enough cash, you can tell all of your friends that you have the same job that they had. Pretty sweet, right? Not only that, but you have a killer mansion right next to all the great shopping on the Champs-Élysées. Your sixty-thousand-square-foot residence, Hôtel de Pontalba, includes three chefs and a dining room that seats 120 people.[3]

It's so big and lavish that you have plenty of space for those friends who call you up when they're in town looking for a place to crash. For example, when Charles Rivkin was U.S. ambassador to France, Secretary of State Hillary Clinton stayed there.[4] Life is also pretty good for the spouses of the U.S. ambassador to France. As noted in chapter 1, Rivkin's wife was given "closet fairies" to make sure she didn't wear the same outfit twice.[5]

Does this life sound appealing? If so, the closet fairies, the hotel as your house, and the title can all be yours, so long as you donate enough money to a president! Silly Benjamin Franklin and Thomas Jefferson–thinking that ability and competence mattered when it comes to American diplomats. All you need to become a U.S. ambassador today is a fat bank account.

Political Spoils

America's founding fathers would be rolling in their graves if they saw how presidents dole out titles to their friends in exchange for campaign money.

Our government may not name you a duke, but with enough money, you can be given a diplomatic post.

Washington now hands out ambassadorships like (very expensive) candy. During President Bill Clinton's time in office, 28 percent of his nominees for ambassadorial posts were political appointees–his buddies and benefactors.[6] For President George W. Bush it was 30 percent.[7] In President Obama's first term in office, 37 percent of the ambassadorships were given to political appointees.[8] In his second term, 53 percent.[9] During Obama's tenure as president his nominees for ambassadorships gave more than $13 million to him and his Democratic allies.[10] And these political appointees don't have to worry about being placed in high-risk locations. The president makes sure to nominate them to posts in stable countries in western Europe or the Caribbean.

Two economists from Pennsylvania State University calculated the implicit price tag of the U.S. ambassador title, in terms of presidential donations. They found that the more money people bundled for the president, the more likely they would get a desirable posting in a stable country with high tourism and high gross domestic product. If a wealthy friend of the president forked over $550,000 or bundled over $750,000, he or she had a 90 percent chance of landing one of the coveted posts in western Europe.[11] If the friend wants to go to Paris and become U.S. ambassador to France like Benjamin Franklin once was, the aspiring diplomat has to give $1.1 million. But if he or she bundles $616,940, that'll work, too.

And what about the most sought-after location, London? According to the study, you have to spend somewhere between $650,000 and $2.3 million to land the glamorous post.[12] So when the queen of the fashion world set her eyes on the Court of St. James's, she didn't need to study up on Anglo-American relations or develop a reputation for diplomacy. All she needed to do was open up her checkbook.

The Ambassador Wears Prada

Anna Wintour is *Vogue* magazine's editor in chief and arguably the most powerful woman in the fashion world. She is known for her undiplomatic and cold demeanor, earning her the nickname "Nuclear Wintour." Her notoriously unapproachable and frosty behavior inspired the book (and later the film) *The Devil Wears Prada,* about an awful fashion magazine editor who treats people terribly. With a reputation like that, you would think there is no way in the world Anna Wintour would ever be considered for a job in diplomacy.

But the truth is that if you're willing to help raise a ton of money for the winning campaign, your lack of qualifications and your reputation as a terrible person can be overlooked.

In 2011 and 2012, Anna Wintour not only held $32,400-a-plate fundraisers at her New York City residence, but she bundled a total of $2.6 million.[13] She also helped put together a fundraising effort for Obama called "Runway to Win." The fashion line designed by top designers and celebrities ended up bringing in $40 million for the president. Wintour expected one thing in return for all of her efforts: the U.S. ambassadorship in London.

Despite Wintour's clear lack of diplomacy, President Obama put her in the running for the post, even though the position requires cultivating personal relationships. (What could go wrong?) But, in the end, the plum position ended up going to Obama's chief fundraiser, Matthew Barzun. Wintour may have raised a lot of money for Obama, but Barzun chaired Obama's money team. When it comes to becoming a U.S. ambassador, it goes to the highest bidder.

America's Princess

Some people are nominated or put on a short list for a U.S. ambassadorship for reasons other than money, like in the case of Caroline Kennedy. Turns out, if you're already part of the American royal class, you can get a diplomatic post simply for writing an op-ed.

When Senator Barack Obama was running against Hillary Clinton for president, he was trailing her in the polls and didn't have the name recognition and credibility that she had among Democrats. Obama needed a boost, so he turned to the daughter of President John F. Kennedy, Caroline Kennedy. She helped him out by endorsing him in the *New York Times* with an op-ed titled "A President Like My Father."

"I have never had a president who inspired me the way people tell me that my father inspired them," Kennedy wrote in her op-ed. "But for the first time, I believe I have found the man who could be that president—not just for me, but for a new generation of Americans."

It was a huge moment. One of the most powerful American royal families was supporting Senator Barack Obama over another American dynasty—the Clintons. Kennedy went on to speak at the Democratic National Convention, calling Obama "the kind of leader my father wrote about in *Profiles in Courage*" (a comment so preposterous that it seems unlikely she ever read *Profiles in Courage,* which may be one of the only things she has in common with her father). Four years later, Kennedy even cochaired Obama's reelection campaign.

The Camelot heiress's endorsement was the first presidential endorsement she has ever made for someone who wasn't a Kennedy, and her Obama crush didn't go unrewarded. The president nominated her to become U.S. ambassador to Japan, even though she had no experience in government, no experience in diplomacy, and no experience with Japan.

Kennedy's résumé is even thinner than her father's was when his bootlegger daddy bought him a House seat. But when you are a part of the royal class and you help out those in power, it doesn't matter if you have zero experience. In October 2013 the Democratic-controlled U.S. Senate confirmed Caroline Kennedy to replace the equally unqualified John Roos, who had "earned" the job by raising money for Barack Obama.

Norway: "Total Ignorance"

During the Obama administration, many unqualified, wealthy individuals have been nominated to become ambassadors as a thank-you from the president. For example, in 2014, President Obama nominated the CEO of Chartwell Hotels, George Tsunis, to be the U.S. ambassador to Norway. The hotel magnate happens to be a big backer of both President Obama and the Democratic Party. He donated more than $250,000 to the Democratic Party in 2012 and over $278,000 in 2010.[14] Tsunis has no connection to Norway and has no background in government, but that didn't matter to President Obama.

When it came time for Tsunis's confirmation hearing,

things didn't go very well. One would expect that Tsunis would come into the hearing with at the very least a basic understanding of Norway's history and politics, but apparently that's asking too much from our appointed ambassadors.

During the hearing Senator John McCain asked Tsunis about Norway's anti-immigration party, the Progress Party. Tsunis responded nervously and characterized the Progress Party as extreme and part of the fringe element in Norway. He also described the Progress Party as one that "spewed hatred." The Progress Party in Norway is actually not a fringe element but a major party.

As the hearing continued, Tsunis dug himself deeper and deeper into a hole by admitting that, despite wanting to lead America's mission in Norway, he had never been to Norway. To make matters worse (as if that were possible) he described the country as having a president and being a republic. But there is just a little problem: Norway has a king and a prime minister.

Before the hearing was over, Tsunis had lost credibility, embarrassed the United States, and disrespected an entire country. The U.S. embassy in Norway had to formally apologize to the people of the country and to the mainstream (not fringe) Progress Party. The Norway Progress Party demanded an apology from President Obama for choosing such an ignorant person as a potential ambassador, and the Norwegian paper the *Local* called Tsunis's testimony a "faltering, incoherent performance" where he displayed "total ignorance." Norwegian Americans wrote op-eds and organized to try to get members of Congress to vote against his confirmation.[15]

After much pressure, Tsunis realized that maybe diplomacy isn't really his thing and withdrew his nomination.

Argentina: "I've Traveled Pretty Extensively" . . . Just Not to Argentina

Noah Bryson Mamet is very rich. His background is in political consulting and raising lots of cash for Democrats. When Barack Obama ran for president, Mamet persuaded his rich friends to give the candidate at least half a million dollars. In return, Obama named him ambassador to Argentina.[16]

During his confirmation hearing Mamet was asked whether he had ever visited Argentina. "I haven't had the opportunity yet to be there," he said. "I've traveled pretty extensively around the world. But I haven't yet had a chance."

On top of never setting foot in the country that he was going to be ambassador of, he didn't even speak the language of the country! You would expect Spanish fluency to be a job requirement. Shouldn't our ambassador be able to deliver America's message to the people and government of Argentina in their native language?

Yes, Argentina is a plum post, but the country is also dealing with currency devaluation, an issue that certainly has the potential to turn into a national crisis. Someone with an experienced background who can articulate America's interests (in Spanish!) ought to be placed there, not just someone who helped out the president. But when it comes to giving out titles in Washington, a checkbook supersedes qualifications.

The Senate voted 50 to 43 to confirm Mamet's nomination.

Hungary: I Wanna Be a Producer, er, an Ambassador

Colleen Bell was nominated to be the ambassador of Hungary. Her background? She was a producer for the soap opera *The Bold and the Beautiful* and, more important, a half-a-million-dollar bundler for President Obama.[17]

When it comes to the latest love triangles and betrayals happening on *The Bold and the Beautiful,* Colleen Bell is all caught up. But when it came to the country of Hungary–she knew very little.

During her hearing, Bell couldn't even articulate America's interests in the central European country where she wanted to become U.S. ambassador:

SENATOR McCAIN: So what would you be doing
      differently from your predecessor, who obviously
      had very rocky relations with the present
      government?
MS. BELL: If confirmed, I look forward to working with
      the broad range of society–
SENATOR McCAIN: My question was, what would you do
      differently?

MS. BELL: Senator, in terms of what I would do
     differently from my predecessor, Kounalakis–
SENATOR MCCAIN: That's the question.
MS. BELL: Well, what I would like to do when–if
     confirmed, I would like to work toward engaging
     civil society in a deeper . . . in a deeper–
SENATOR MCCAIN: Obviously, you don't want to answer
     my question.

Despite McCain's protest against the appointment, the Senate confirmed Bell by a vote of 52 to 42.

The Bahamas: A 276-Day Vacation

Nicole Avant is another one of President Obama's not-so-qualified appointees. She is the daughter of music executive Clarence Avant. With her husband, Ted Sarandos, the chief content officer at Netflix, Avant became Obama's top Hollywood fundraiser, hosting fancy shindigs for him and bundling millions of dollars.

Obama rewarded Avant by appointing her U.S. ambassador to the Bahamas. The Bahamas post may sound plum, but it's critical, especially when it comes to combating human trafficking, drug running, and other illegal activity. A professional should have been placed there, but instead Obama chose to appoint someone who had no diplomatic experience.

Like many of these wealthy presidential bundlers, Avant didn't care about doing the job. So it's no surprise that according to a State Department inspector general's report on the U.S. embassy in the Bahamas, Avant was lousy at her job.

The report stated, "The embassy is recovering from an extended period of dysfunctional leadership and mismanagement, which has caused problems throughout the embassy. Critical security upgrades in embassy housing were not made, and the U.S. Government paid rent for 2 years on a vacant consular agency office in the Turks and Caicos Islands."[18]

Considering that the Bahamas are sunny, warm, and beautiful, Avant spent surprisingly little time there. Instead, she would fly back to her hometown in California. When she was actually in the Bahamas she worked from home and wanted to have little interaction with the agency.

According to the inspector general's report,

> The Ambassador had not had frequent policy-level interaction with the Department or other Washington agencies. At the beginning of her tenure, she relied unduly on her former DCM [Deputy Chief of Mission] to attend to day-to-day contacts with the desk and other offices in the Department. Interviews in Washington likewise revealed that the front office of the Bureau of Western Hemisphere Affairs and other Washington agencies were not in regular contact with the Ambassador about the conduct of her mission. This lack of regular contact contributed to the Ambassador's sense of isolation from the Department.[19]

From November 2009 to September 2011, Avant missed 276 days of work. The inspector general concluded that her extensive travel out of country and preference to work from the ambassador's residence for a significant portion of the workday contributed to a perception of indifference. . . . The frequent absences of the ambassador contributed to poor mission management.[20]

Belgium: Only "Traditional Anti-Semitism . . . Should Be Condemned"

Avant isn't the only bundler who caused a bundle of trouble by being a lousy ambassador. She's joined in that category by Howard Gutman, who was awarded the position of U.S. ambassador to Belgium after helping to raise at least half a million dollars for President Obama.[21]

While ambassador, Howard Gutman spoke at a European Jewish Union conference on anti-Semitism. He told the room of attendees that it's Israel's fault that Muslims don't like Jewish people. "A distinction should be made between traditional anti-Semitism, which should be condemned, and Muslim hatred for Jews, which stems from the ongoing conflict between Israel and the Palestinians," he said.[22] He also argued that if Israel could come to an agreement with Palestine, there would be less Muslim anti-Semitism.

While Gutman's jaw-dropping statements understandably stunned the room filled with Jewish lawyers from all over Europe,[23] America shouldn't be surprised. This is what happens when Washington politicians appoint people for being a wealthy buddy of the president.

Luxembourg: "The Office of Medical
Services Should Send Medical
Professionals to Embassy Luxembourg
to Evaluate . . . Staff"

In 2009, President Obama nominated wealthy philanthropist
and arts advocate Cynthia Stroum to become U.S. ambassador to Luxembourg. Of course, Stroum had no background
in government, but she landed the job because of her support
for President Obama. She'd bundled more than $800,000 for
the president.[24]

Stroum's performance as ambassador once again illustrates why it's a terrible idea for presidents to appoint
non-career diplomats in exchange for campaign donations.
According to an inspector general's report, "the Ambassador's confrontational management style, chronic gaps in
senior and other staffing caused by curtailments, and the ab-
sence of a sense of direction have brought major elements of
Embassy Luxembourg to a state of dysfunction."[25]

Stroum's problems started when she first arrived at her
residence in Luxembourg. You would think that she would be
thrilled to be living in the beautiful and lavish mansion. But
Ambassador Stroum demands the best, and the residence
didn't meet her high standards. In particular, according to
the report, Stroum was "not pleased with the condition of
the [residence's] mattress, and preferred a queen bed to the
king-size bed already provided."[26]

Because she didn't like the king-size mattress, she decided

to purchase a new one and attempted to bill Uncle Sam. Her request was denied. She was told it was a personal expense and would not be covered by tax dollars. Stroum wasn't satisfied, so she tried again in 2010 to get reimbursed for her mattress. The request was once again denied. Later, the acting deputy mission chief eventually broke the rules and issued a voucher for Stroum's reimbursement.

Now that her mattress situation was solved, it was on to the bathrooms! She wanted them to be refurbished and updated. She delegated the task of remodeling the bathrooms to her small staff at the Luxembourg embassy. In the meantime, Stroum wanted to stay in a temporary residence for six months.

According to the IG report, one of the local employees

spent virtually all of his time over a 6-week period searching for a temporary CMR [Chief of Mission Residence]. He and other members of the general services staff worked with real estate agents and his contacts in Luxembourg, Belgium, Germany, and France to find landlords who were willing to rent a suitable temporary residence during the 6-month renovation of the permanent CMR. He and the management officer screened 200 residences and visited 30–40 houses and apartments in Luxembourg. Two officials from Embassy Brussels also traveled to Luxembourg to assist with the search. Based on the Ambassador's requirements, all but four residences were deemed unsuitable; the Ambassador rejected all four.[27]

Not only did the ambassador waste the time of the staff members (and the hard-earned money of taxpayers), but she also treated her associates terribly. According to the report, Stroum's tenure as ambassador "was fraught with personality conflicts, verbal abuse and questionable expenditures on travel, wine and liquor."[28]

To give you an idea of how awful Stroum was . . . many of her staffers either quit or tried to get transfers to Iraq and Afghanistan.[29]

The ones who stayed around didn't end up in great shape.

Stroum's behavior toward her staff was so bad that the IG recommended medical attention for the staff. He wrote that Stroum was "aggressive, bullying, hostile, and intimidating" and that "the Office of Medical Services should send medical professionals to Embassy Luxembourg to evaluate morale and stress levels of staff."[30]

At the end of 2010, Stroum had money left over in the budget. Instead of returning the unused tax dollars to the government, she spent it purchasing tons of booze.

When Stroum's cook was fired, she was determined to hire a professional. Without proper authorization, Stroum took $2,400 from the program funds to fly herself and another employee to Switzerland to find a new cook. They went to a professional school there that trains people for employment at places such as Buckingham Palace.[31]

Stroum was a disaster, so Obama went back to his little black bundler book and found Robert Mandell, the CEO of a real estate company. Mandell had no diplomatic experience, but he gave more than $30,000 to President Obama's campaign and $50,000 to his inauguration committee.[32] He was confirmed by the Senate and replaced Stroum in 2011.

Embassy Suites: Neglect in Benghazi, Opulence in London

Imagine that you are a security guard at America's diplomatic post in Benghazi, Libya, on the evening of September 11, 2012. You hear gunfire and a loud explosion. You look at the security camera that's positioned at the main gate in front of the compound. It shows a large group of militants headed in through the gate.[33] You hit the alarm.

The heavily armed Islamists shoot at the buildings and set fire to the main building. The U.S. ambassador in Benghazi, Christopher Stevens, runs to a safe room, along with informational management officer Sean Smith. Stevens calls Gregory Hicks, the deputy mission chief in Libya.

"Greg," he says, "we're under attack."

Stevens is initially protected in the safe room, but the Islamists set fire to the building and drop mortars on the roof.

Within hours, Ambassador Stevens, Sean Smith, and two former Navy SEALs are dead.

Independent reviews of the events in Benghazi have concluded that the attacks and the tragic deaths could have been prevented had there been adequate security. The State Department's review of the attack concluded that the security at the facility before and on the day of the attack was substandard "despite repeated requests" from the Benghazi post for more security.[34] The report added that the security was "inadequate for Benghazi and grossly inadequate to deal with the attack that took place."[35]

You would think that in a high-risk location like Benghazi the State Department would make the facility as protected as possible. But in a sign of just how unserious the State Department was about its responsibilities to protect our diplomats there, a surveillance camera system had been sent to the Benghazi post, but the State Department never bothered to send in a team to install it.

The lack of security was because State Department officials considered Benghazi simply a temporary post, so they waived the security requirements. According to Eric Nordstrom, the regional security officer stationed in Libya during the time of the attacks, the volatile country was one of the few diplomatic posts that were considered high-risk in every single threat category. But the Benghazi post never met the requirements that are set by the Overseas Security Policy Board.

"We did not meet any of those standards with the exception of perhaps the height of the wall," said Nordstrom, speaking before Congress. In written testimony, Nordstrom explained:

According to the Government Accountability Office (GAO), six threat categories inform the [Security Environment Threat List]: international terrorism, indigenous terrorism political violence, crime, human intelligence, and technical threat. A rating is then assigned for each category, on a four-level scale.

- Critical: grave impact on American diplomats
- High: serious impact on American diplomats
- Medium: moderate impact on American diplomats
- Low: minor impact on American diplomats

The protective measures for each post are dictated by the post's overall threat level.

The . . . requirements . . . standards, and . . . ratings are the critical foundation for all [Regional Security Offices] and Posts on which security measures are evaluated and deficiencies identified. At the time of the Benghazi attack, only a small number of the 264 overseas diplomatic posts were rated either HIGH or CRITICAL in threat categories related to political violence, terrorism, and crime. Our posts in Benghazi and Tripoli were among those posts and the only two facilities that met no . . . standards. Furthermore, Benghazi and Tripoli were not located in a country where the Department of State could count on effective support or response from the host nation—a fact that was clearly and repeatedly reported to policy makers in Washington, DC.[36]

Since the Benghazi post was given "non-status" (due to it being a temporary facility), the security requirements were waived and resources were difficult to obtain to protect what was one of the State Department's most vulnerable and critical posts. Instead agency officials were busy putting together plans to make the State Department's most plum diplomatic post even more lavish and desirable.

In 2012, the State Department unveiled a big surprise it had been working on: a plan for a new over-the-top $1 billion embassy in London. The new London embassy will be a crystal embassy, will span 500,000 square feet, and will be completed in 2017.

The exterior of the embassy will be made of energy-absorbing material. The roof will have solar panels and will be transparent in order to allow for views of the city. It will feature a pond, a park, and gardens on each floor of the building and will be the most expensive embassy ever built. One of the biggest reasons for the high cost of the embassy is the glass design, which the State Department recommended scrapping due to the exorbitant cost. The glass is made in Europe but needs to be shipped to America for framing and then shipped back to Europe—because when it comes to using other people's money for embassies inhabited by the wealthy and well-connected, only the best type of glass will suffice.[37]

This just shows the priorities of our government. They weren't concerned about Benghazi because Benghazi isn't a post that has an extremely wealthy individual who bundled money for the president. There was no glitzy Hollywood producer in Benghazi. Instead the people who get sent to high-risk areas like Benghazi are people who have their jobs because they work hard, are talented, and typically aren't part of the ruling class. This is a damaging example of what happens when our government values people because of their wealth and status, and prioritizes the needs of the wealthy over the needs of America.

The Dangers of Ambassadorship Auctions

Washington's system of awarding ambassadorships to the wealthy friends of the royal class is clearly a recipe for disaster. It serves no one except the president and his friends and risks jeopardizing our strategic interests. The role of a U.S. ambassador is important–he or she is intimately involved in delicate negotiations and is the go-to person if an emergency arises. Our ambassadors should, at the very minimum, be familiar with the nation where they're going to be ambassador, and should be able to handle the pressure of a confirmation hearing.

The practice has been especially appalling in recent years, because President Obama promised a different kind of governance. He said our country's prestige was waning, and he promised to restore it. He said our allies were insulted, and he promised to respect them. Before he took office, he said Washington was a place for the wealthy and the powerful, and he promised to return it to the people.

Instead, Obama's ambassadors have further injured America's credibility, repeatedly insulted our allies, and symbolized Washington cronyism at its crudest and crassest–by engaging in the same behavior as monarchies and banana republics.

This practice sends a bad message to the bright and talented diplomats in America who have diligently served our country for years. They work selflessly in dangerous areas around the world, and repeatedly get passed over for top positions in stable countries. And if they do get appointed to a plum location, they are forced to work under unqualified individuals who got the job simply because they raised money for the president. The practice lowers morale in the Foreign Service and discourages all of the hardworking diplomats who have earned their positions. It's unfair that our long-serving diplomats who want to one day become ambassadors can aspire only to be one in the most dangerous countries in the world.

Awarding ambassadorships to the wealthy can also have disastrous consequences for America. The Washington elite argue that it's not a big deal because they aren't sending these political appointees to troubled areas. But what if a crisis were to break out? Are we really willing to roll the dice and have someone in place who is unqualified, as opposed to having a trained professional to deal with managing the crisis? If a crisis were to break out in western Europe or the Caribbean—there is, after all, some precedent—do we really want to leave America's response in the hands of a television producer, whose expertise is in putting together television shows?

When critics were blasting Caroline Kennedy's appointment as U.S. ambassador to Japan, Kurt Campbell, the former assistant secretary of state for east Asian and Pacific affairs, said that "what you really want in an ambassador is someone who can get the president of the United States on the phone. . . . I can't think of anybody in the United States who could do that more quickly than Caroline Kennedy."[38]

But this is nonsense. Giving people ambassadorships simply because they have access to the president just leads to ambassadors becoming nothing more than flacks and pawns for the White House. Our foreign policy decisions ought to be made with our national interests in mind and crafted with help of expert advice from various departments and agencies. When you have ambassadors who are invested in the president's political future, they're viewing things from the point of view of "What's good for the president?" instead of "What's good for America?"

Selling ambassadorships is also insulting to our friends and allies. It signals to our allies that we don't consider the job of U.S. ambassador in their country important, so we're sending amateurs rather than real professionals. It also diminishes the role of an ambassador, a role that used to be reserved for our greatest statesmen.

When it was revealed that Anna Wintour wouldn't get the ambassador post in London, her friend the fashion designer Oscar de La Renta came to her defense. De la Renta tried to lessen the blow by saying that Wintour wasn't upset about being passed over because she didn't really want the ambassador post. He told *Women's Wear Daily* that Wintour didn't care that much because "ambassadors were great in the eighteenth century. Today, it's going to the opening of a cafeteria."

Because presidents have reduced ambassadorships to nothing more than favors for the favored, there is, sadly, far too much truth in that analysis.

CHAPTER 10

Taking Back
Our Country

Citizen Legislator

George McGovern served for twenty-four years in high office as a leading liberal voice. He was a congressman, a U.S.
senator from South Dakota, a John F. Kennedy ally, and the
Democratic Party's presidential nominee in 1972. His presidential ambitions, however, were squandered when he was
defeated in a landslide by Republican Richard Nixon. Despite
his crushing defeat, McGovern never strayed from his deep
liberal roots. His political career was marked by a devotion
to liberal policies. While in office he was supportive of policies of intervening in the free market. And when he decided
to leave his political career, he followed the path of many before and after him—he joined the lucrative speaking circuit.

   After accumulating a healthy chunk of money from speaking engagements, he decided to leave the Washington bubble

behind him. He saved the speaking fees he had generated
and entered the real world. He purchased a forty-three-year
lease on a 150-room hotel in Stratford, Connecticut,[1] finally
fulfilling his "longtime dream to own a combination hotel,
restaurant and public conference facility–complete with an
experienced manager and staff."[2]

But just three years later, McGovern filed for bankruptcy.
The liberal regulations that he was in favor of as a member of
Congress crippled his small business.

Looking back at his time in Congress he said: "In retro-
spect, I wish I had known more about the hazards and difficulties of such a business, especially during a recession of the
kind that hit New England just as I was acquiring the inn's
forty-three-year leasehold. I also wish that during the years
I was in public office, I had had this firsthand experience
about the difficulties business people face every day. That
knowledge would have made me a better U.S. senator and a
more understanding presidential contender."

He had realized that the regulatory state, which he was in
favor of while in office, was terrible for American businesses.
Although his support for regulations was motivated by good
intentions, he didn't have enough private sector experience
to foresee the unintended consequences of these policies. It
wasn't until he left Washington and entered into the private
sector that he realized that "the 'one-size-fits-all' rules for
business ignore the reality of the marketplace."[3] He also
realized that "setting thresholds for regulatory guidelines
at artificial levels–e.g., 50 employees or more, $500,000
in sales–takes no account of other realities, such as profit

margins, labor intensive vs. capital intensive businesses, and local market economics."[4] McGovern's experience is a perfect example of why career politicians are terrible for our country.

Sadly, his story isn't unique. Many politicians in Washington have little to no background in the private sector. They have spent so much of their career in the public sphere that it's impossible for them to fathom how their legislation may hurt average folks in the real world. Many of their policies sound good on paper in Washington, D.C., but are destructive when they're forced onto businesses across America.

But this is not how it was supposed to be. Public service is supposed to be a temporary gig, not a permanent one. Our founding fathers envisioned a citizen legislature, not a Washington of career politicians. If you were to hop into a time machine and ask our founding fathers whether they are concerned about political careerism, they would look at you confused. In fact, they probably wouldn't even be able to fathom the idea that people in America would want to be in political office for their entire lives. During the early days of our country, the areas in which government operated were undesirable areas to live. Being a public servant back then was vastly different: The pay was poor, it was hard work, there were few benefits or perks, and the federal government's power was limited. The only reason people would get involved in politics was that they truly were interested in serving their nation.

There was also the tradition of self-imposed term limits, which they felt was necessary in order to be a good public servant. One of our founding fathers, Roger Sherman, who helped draft the Declaration of Independence, argued that "representatives ought to return home and mix with the people. By remaining at the seat of government, they would acquire the habits of the place, which might differ from those of their constituents." Sherman, like our other founders, didn't believe in people serving long terms. In fact, term limits were included in the Articles of Confederation. The founders chose to leave the topic out of the U.S. Constitution because they viewed it as "entering into too much detail."[5] But it was understood that, in order to be a good public servant, term limits were necessary.

Today, self-imposed term limits are a concept rarely mentioned in Washington. Chapman University professor Ronald Rotunda has pointed that the "turnover in the House of Lords has been greater than the turnover in the House of Representatives. There was even more turnover in the membership of the Soviet Politburo."[6]

Consequently, we don't have a citizen legislature like our founders envisioned. Instead, we have a legislature made up of career politicians like George McGovern, who are constantly implementing policies that apply to us, without understanding the damaging effects. According to Benjamin Franklin, "In free governments, the rulers are the servants, and the people their superiors. . . . For the former to return among the latter does not degrade, but promote them."[7] When politicians know they must return to regular life and live under the laws they try to pass, they'll have more skin in the game and will be more thoughtful when crafting policy.

Term limits would help our members understand the people they represent. Most Americans don't work in Washington, D.C., their entire lives. They don't get amazing perks from taxpayers, nor do they socialize at cocktail parties in Georgetown. That's not America. So why do we continue to send these people back to Washington to live these lavish lives? Let's demand term limits. There needs to be an infusion of new blood and more legislative turnover. We're allowing these out-of-touch individuals to rule over us for however long they like, while we suckers pay for all of their perks.

Some opponents of term limits argue that this will get rid of our most experienced legislators, the ones who have expertise in important areas. But right now that's what we have—a government with "experienced legislators." What has that gotten us? Trillions of dollars in debt, high unemployment, and an entitlement state that's bursting at the seams. Further, when members have been in Congress for a long time they're more likely to get a better understanding of how to abuse the system. There is more corruption and they have more power. Members of Congress who have been serving for a substantial amount of time are the ones who get seats on key committees and control the legislative agenda. Therefore, when there is fresh, new blood, there is very little the newcomers can actually get done.

Polls show that Americans are overwhelmingly in favor of limiting the time politicians are in office, yet term limits is rarely a topic discussed during political races. It's incumbent on Americans to elect members of Congress who believe in term limits. Just as we weigh our candidates' thoughts on the economy, healthcare, and a wide array of other issues, we ought to weigh their views on term limits.

Our representatives are becoming career politicians who are more interested in getting reelected and helping themselves than actually working to help America. If we had term limits it would fundamentally change the incentives for people seeking office and alter their priorities when they are in office. We need to clean up Washington and return our government to what our founders originally intended, which was a government made up of citizen legislators, not career politicians. We don't need a permanent ruling class in Washington; what we need to do is give Washington the reality check it deserves.

Stop Insider Trading

Being a public servant should be about sacrifice, not about enriching oneself. Our public officials have lost the trust of the American people because public service is more focused on the latter. One of the first steps in restoring the American people's trust is to eliminate insider trading.

If one wants to be a public servant, well, then, one should understand that sacrifices must be made. One of those sacrifices is that the assets of congresspeople should be placed in a blind trust. Therefore, the members' stocks and bonds would be managed by someone else whom they have no contact with. It's unacceptable that members of Congress get to Washington, D.C., with middle-class incomes and walk out filthy rich.

Blind trusts are not unprecedented. Presidents have had blind trusts. Many critics are quick to point out that a flaw in a blind trust plan is that sometimes it's not actually blind. For example, President Lyndon B. Johnson was able to make tons of money because he had a family friend and two of his business associates run the trust.[8] With our elected officials, this can't happen. We should demand that all members and cabinet members place their assets in a trust that is run by someone who isn't a relative or a friend. Further, there should be zero communication between the beneficiary and the people who manage the trust. It should be called public service for a reason.

End Congressional Pensions

When Republican Thomas Massie of Kentucky was elected to the House of Representatives, he did something unheard of: he rejected the comfy congressional pension offered to members of Congress. Massie still must pay into the Federal Employees Retirement System, but declined the benefits that are guaranteed to members of Congress.

The pension system given to members of Congress is grossly superior to what most Americans receive. While pensions are now becoming a thing of the past for most Americans, members of Congress are living awfully well, thanks to their employer-match plan. Furthermore, they don't even have the same retirement age as average Americans! Representatives and senators can receive a pension after only five years of service at the age of sixty-two. If they have completed twenty years of service they can receive their pension at the age of fifty. In 2011, almost three hundred former members of Congress received annual pensions of over $70,000.[9] If a member of Congress serves only five years, he or she is guaranteed a pension of over $14,000.[10] What about Speaker John Boehner? Now that he's retiring, he's eligible for an annual pension worth over $85,000. The current plan not only is a waste of taxpayer dollars but also incentivizes people in Congress to make a career out of being a politician.

Massie tells me that he believes it's unfair to taxpayers, which is why he coauthored the controversial End Pensions in Congress Act. The bill would essentially dismantle the current pension program. It would make it so that current members of Congress who have served less than five years, and future members of Congress, will not be given a pension. Instead, our public servants will have to save for retirement, and rely on 401(k)-type plans rather than relying on taxpayers. Basically, they'll have to live like the rest of us.

The cost of providing federal employees and our members of Congress with comfy pension plans is costing taxpayers. The Civil Service Retirement System's unfunded liability has jumped to over $700 billion.[11] The Federal Employees Retirement System has $20.1 billion dollars in unfunded liabilities.[12]

Not only is this an unsustainable path, but it also serves as just another way for our servant class to enrich themselves. During our country's infancy, Benjamin Franklin delivered a speech at the Constitutional Convention of 1787 arguing that high government officials shouldn't receive a salary. He believed "that the pleasure of doing good and serving their country, and the respect such conduct entitles them to, are sufficient motives." He argued that some may believe "that this is a Utopian idea, and that we can never find men to serve us in the executive department without paying them well for their services. I conceive this to be a mistake." By offering people perks and salaries he feared that the "government of the states may, in future times, end in a monarchy."[13]

So how did America go from believing a salary alone was extravagant to now providing six-figure pensions? We have strayed so far from the ideals of the heroic men who fought and risked their lives to create this great nation. It's time we stand up and do something about it.

Ending congressional pensions is a step in the right direction. Why should the taxpayers fund a comfy perk for members of Congress that only incentivizes politicians to stay in power for as long as possible? It's benefits like this that attract the worst kinds of people to Washington. Public service shouldn't be a guaranteed path to riches, and we shouldn't allow our country to turn into the monarchy that Benjamin Franklin feared America could become. It's not too late to turn back the clock.

Restore Fiscal Sanity

In 2011, former Texas governor Rick Perry was running for the Republican presidential nomination. During one of the debates, the governor began naming off the agencies that he wanted to get rid of. The problem was that Perry

couldn't remember all of the agencies he wanted to eliminate. The cringeworthy moment went viral. The department
he couldn't remember was the Department of Energy. His
critics seized the moment to point out that Perry was not
very smart—how could he forget the government agency he
wanted to get rid of?

But the moment was actually reflective of what's wrong
with our government. There are so many federal government agencies that should be eliminated, how could you
fault the guy for forgetting which one he wanted to get rid
of? Our own government doesn't even know how many agencies it has![14]

I decided to try to find out how many government agencies and offices exist by calling the Government Accountability Office, the agency responsible for examining the
money that all federal government agencies spend. If the
GAO is responsible for overseeing how the U.S. government
spends taxpayer dollars, then it surely should have a list of all
the offices and agencies!

But when I called the GAO I was told that it actually didn't
have that information. The GAO then referred me to the Office of Management and Budget. The OMB then told me that
I would have to contact the Government Accountability Office for that information.

It was clear they didn't have a list. The fact that the government can't keep track of all of its agencies and offices
shows just how monstrous it has become. And when the government is large—especially this large—it breeds corruption.
Because the bigger the government, the more money that bu-

reaucrats control, making it easier for them to spend or use money in unsavory ways.

Our government is so big that there are countless programs in the U.S. government that overlap. For example, the U.S. government has twelve (twelve!) of the same programs, in different government departments, that will pay for you to get to your doctor's appointment.[15] Also, the government has two different agencies, the Environmental Protection Agency and the Food and Drug Administration, that inspect the exact same laboratories.[16] Sadly, these aren't anomalies; these duplicate programs often go unnoticed because of the monstrous size of the government.

These, literally, countless agencies are made up of bureaucrats enforcing and creating rules and regulations that only harm the average American. In 2014 alone, the cost of regulation was $2 trillion, which costs Americans $1.88 trillion in lost productivity.[17]

Not only are these regulations a waste of taxpayer dollars, but they also create ample opportunity for corruption. When you give government the power to disperse tons of rules, subsidies, and exemptions it often leads to government workers giving preferential treatment to their business friends.

American voters from all sides of the aisle want to reduce corruption in the political system. They complain about the influence peddling, and the money flowing from private enterprise to the government. But many of the solutions they propose consist of creating new agencies and rules, which only increase the role and size of the government. So many fail to realize that all of the influence peddling and corporate money is often the result of having a big government. Instead of making the government more active, let's slash the size of the government.

If you keep the government small, there will be fewer federal jobs, limited money, and less opportunity to abuse the system. Every single time we increase the size of government, we're increasing the cash that flows through the government and creating fresh opportunities for waste and corruption. Similarly, with every regulation and government program, there is an abundance of temptation. What ends up happening is that businesses respond to regulations by sending cash to Washington in order to influence, or bribe, policy makers to exempt them from these rules and regulations. The wealthy and powerful businesses get exempted, and the small guys who can't open up a lobbying shop in the Beltway get hurt. The more regulations there are, the more private companies compete for government favors. This influence peddling is inevitable and continues to get worse because of the vast number of regulations that, oftentimes, are unnecessary. If Americans want less corruption and waste, then they need to demand a simplification of our government and a reduction in its size and power.

We as American citizens are responsible for guarding our republic and keeping government officials in check and responsive to our needs. It's incumbent on the people to hold the government accountable, but how can the American people hold government officials accountable when the number of government officials, departments, agencies is so vast? Many people are quick to criticize American voters for the corruption in Washington by saying they ought to pay more attention to government officials. While Americans certainly ought to pay more attention, it's an impossible task for them. How in the world can we American voters keep our officials in check when we're dealing with a government as vast as ours? The federal government employs more than 2.7 million people (not counting non-civilian military personnel).[18] If we want to limit corruption, let's limit the power of politicians and the size of the government.

Restraining Lobbying

When people think of lobbyists, the image of someone with a cigar in a fancy D.C. steakhouse slipping a senator some cash in exchange for a favor is usually what comes to mind. Americans view lobbying as having a bad influence on America, but completely banning lobbying isn't likely. Our right to petition the government is protected by the First Amendment, so our only option is to minimize lobbying as much as possible. So I decided to talk to the most powerful lobbyist in America to figure out whether that's possible.

Grover Norquist is the president and founder of Americans for Tax Reform, a taxpayer advocacy group that works to keep taxes low and simple. His work at ATR has made him "the most powerful non-elected person in Washington."[19]

The most powerful lobbyist in America must know how to end lobbying, right?

I met with Norquist at the ATR offices in Washington to find out how to weaken lobbyists. He told me he believes that there are two kinds of lobbying in Washington, one that works for the taxpayer and for the good of the nation, and one that works to take money from the taxpayer.

"Lobbying in self-defense is legitimate," said Norquist. "Lobbying the government to ask the government to steal other people's money is corrupt." The problem, though, is that what most lobbyists do goes against the interests of the taxpayer. According to Norquist, making the government smaller is key to putting a stop to that and protecting the taxpayer.

"The people who argue against lobbying miss the point," he said. "When the government is small there is very little reason to go pay to get a piece of the action. When there is a lot of money at stake there is no way to fence out those who try to get the money." He helped drive his point home by comparing lobbyists and taxpayer dollars to birthday cake and cockroaches. "Can you imagine somebody saying, 'I'm going to store a birthday cake under the sink and now I'm going to spend fifty years trying to figure out how to keep the cockroaches away from it?' The cockroaches will find their way in!" he said.

The data backs up Norquist's point that more money in the hands of government leads to more lobbying. In the graph on page 253, provided to me by Strategas Research Partners, you'll note that as federal spending goes up, so does lobbying. As federal spending goes down, so does lobbying.

And it makes sense. Everyone who goes to Washington to become a lobbyist is looking to get a piece of the taxpayer pie. If there isn't much pie, there isn't much need for com-

Lobbying Spending & Federal Spending % of GDP

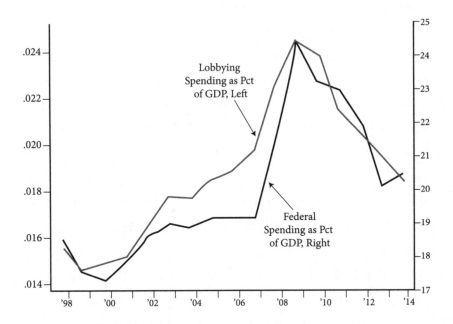

panies and lobbyists to schmooze with politicians to get a piece of it. If we have a government that takes tons of money from taxpayers and has tons of money to dole out, it's going to undoubtedly draw people to try to get a piece of it. If we want to restrain lobbyists and minimize the back-scratching between them and politicians, let's limit the amount of taxpayer dollars they have to negotiate with.

Make Members of Congress Keep Their Day Jobs

When the first Continental Congress met in Philadelphia in 1774, it was a meeting of ordinary Americans—not ambitious career politicians, but farmers, businessmen, lawyers, teachers. They were regular people with full-time jobs who were deeply concerned about their country.

Today, when Congress meets, the room is filled with career politicians who are completely divorced from reality. After being in power so long they begin to look at themselves as regal, rather than as one of the people. Many of them have little private sector experience, and they fly back to their hometowns for only a handful of days each month. They spend so much time in Washington they don't understand the struggles of average Americans. Furthermore, the more time they spend in Congress, the more rules, regulations, and red tape they inflict on average Americans. Today they spend much of their time in Washington attending fancy parties and schmoozing. And when it's time for them to actually get work done, they wait until the very last minute to conduct business and pass budgets. But it wasn't always like this.

So why not return to a part-time Congress? Why not make members of Congress live among their constituents and, more important, live like them? They can be called back to Washington, D.C., for emergency sessions if needed. This will ensure that Congress is filled with people who have real jobs. They can conduct congressional business and hold down regular jobs in their hometowns. It's been done before, and it can be done again.

Some argue that this is impossible and that members of Congress need to work full-time because the government is so big and complex. But we have a full-time Congress now that's milking taxpayers for large staffs and perks. What has that gotten us? The full-time Congress doesn't do anything.

And when they actually do conduct business it's at the very last minute.

Members of Congress should have to return home and to a real job. Our representatives should have to live among the people and deal with the realities of our economy. They should have to work like the rest of us and live under the laws they create. If politicians want to serve "the people," then they should have to live like "the people."

Other Needed Reforms

1. Immediate family members of current members of Congress shouldn't be able to register as lobbyists.

2. When it comes to land deals, members of Congress need to disclose whether they, or a friend or campaign contributor, will benefit from the deal. If so, they should recuse themselves.

3. Whistleblower protections should be granted to congressional staffers so that they can come forward about waste or abuse without fear of retaliation.

4. Stop using taxpayer dollars to subsidize the hair salon and gym for congressional staffers.

5. End double-dipping. Members of Congress should not be able to draw two salaries from taxpayers.

6. End all financial payments for former presidents. All living former presidents are millionaires and are able to do well financially thanks to book deals and speeches.

Embracing Humility

Whenever I read about our founding fathers, I'm always struck by their humility. It's a characteristic that was once valued in our society, but has become virtually extinct. What's happened to it? And is figuring that out the key to cleaning up Washington? David Bobb, author of *Humility: An Unlikely Biography of America's Greatest Virtue,* thinks so. When I spoke to Bobb he made the case that we need to bring back our greatest virtue–the one that helped form America and helped us realize our greatness. It's key to recapturing that greatness.

Our founding fathers understood that humility was necessary for the governance of this great country. It didn't come naturally to them, but it was something they strove for and achieved. They were ambitious, but that ambition was tempered by humility. How is it that America's greatest virtue has now become nonexistent in Washington? The answer is that we simply have stopped electing humble people and instead are continuing to elect people who are more concerned with self-promotion and self-congratulating.

This isn't a policy reform that can be achieved by pressuring those on Capitol Hill to put forth legislation. Rather, it's something that's achievable only through the actions of the American voter. Unfortunately, candidates today are driven to serve this country because they want to enrich themselves. Being able to spot those people when they're on the campaign trail is central. Bobb's advice is to look out for candidates who will not own up to error. Just look at President Obama, for example. He has a history of being unable to acknowledge his mistakes and constantly shifting the blame to someone else. During the aftermath of Benghazi, we were told that he was ignorant of requests from the consulate for additional security.[20] When it came to the VA scandal, he said that he didn't know about it until he saw it on the news.[21] He didn't know that the Obamacare website was going to be a disaster when it launched, despite reports indicating it wasn't ready.[22] When it came to the targeting of conservative groups by the Internal Revenue Service, he said he was unaware, too.[23] Now remember, this is his administration. Not only did he fail to take responsibility as commander in chief, but he chalked these incidents up as simply "phony scandals."

This is something we ought to be looking out for in our public officials. Whenever elections come along we're eager to find out whether a candidate agrees with us on a certain issue (whether it's the economy, healthcare, and so forth). However, it seems as if we care little about the characteristic that helped this country become great: humility.

Voters Need to Wake Up

The size of our government needs to shrink and we need reform, but that's not enough. The solution lies with you. We have an aristocracy in America, and the two royal families—the Clintons and the Bushes—are once again trying to cling to power. If we continue down this path, our founding fathers' work will have been for nothing. They risked their lives to break free from an out-of-touch royal class and monarchy. They laid the groundwork for a healthy republic for us. They made sure to document their thoughts and concerns about the future in the hopes that we would read them and never allow America to become like the aristocratic European countries they detested. But we're headed down the path that they warned us about. Now, more than ever, it's incumbent upon us to remember the spirit of '76 and to put a stop to the royal class they warned us of in their writings.

Our public servants are no longer servants. Instead, they act as though we exist to serve them and their needs. While we work tirelessly each day, they take our money to support their lavish lifestyles. America can no longer afford to subsidize the life of a royal class, nor can it sustain the culture of corruption that has overtaken Washington.

The conditions outlined in this book should serve as a wake-up call, but nothing will change if Americans keep hitting the snooze button and go about their lives as if what's happening in Washington cannot be changed. Fixing our country is dependent on whether the American people are willing to work to hold the royal class in Washington accountable.

There is a story that's often told about Benjamin Franklin leaving Independence Hall on the final day of the Constitutional Convention. Curious citizens gathered outside the hall, eager to learn what kind of government the delegates had settled on. A woman asked Franklin what kind of government they would have. Franklin replied: "A republic, if you can keep it."

More than two hundred years later, Franklin's veiled warning is becoming a reality. We have a ruling class whose members are out of touch with the American people and are solely concerned with enriching themselves. This grand experiment that our founding fathers chose is now in jeopardy. Our government doesn't just rely on the consent of the people; it's dependent on you for its continued health.

We can continue to allow the royal, out-of-touch class in Washington to continue to live lavishly off the backs of taxpayers, or we can hold them accountable and prevent this republic from falling by the wayside. At the end of the day, only you–the voter–can fix Washington. We owe it to ourselves, to America's future generations, and to our heroic founding fathers. Let's work together to preserve their legacy.

NOTES

Chapter 1. An Era of Humility

1. Stanton Lucia, "Dinner Etiquette," Monticello.org, http://www
    .monticello.org/site/research-and-collections/dinner-etiquette.

2. Ibid.

3. Ibid.

4. Ibid.

5. Tom Wolfe, *The Atlantic,* November 1, 2007, http://www.theatlantic
    .com/magazine/archive/2007/11/pell-mell/306312/, accessed
    March 8, 2015.

6. Wayne Whipple, *The Story of the White House* (Philadelphia: Henry
    Altemus Company, 1910).

7. Joseph J. Ellis, *His Excellency: George Washington* (New York: Alfred A.
    Knopf, 2004).

8. Ibid.

9. "George Washington's Resignation Speech," http://msa.maryland.gov/
    msa/stagser/s1259/131/html/gwresign.html.

10. George Washington Papers at the Library of Congress, http://memory
    .loc.gov/ammem/gwhtml/gwhome.html, accessed May 14, 2016.

11. Harvey Sicherman, "Benjamin Franklin: American Diplomacy Tradi-
    tions," November 28, 2008, http://www.unc.edu/depts/diplomat/
    item/2007/0103/sich/sicherman_franklin.html, accessed Novem-
    ber 14, 2014.

12. Ibid.

13. William Haig Miller, James Macaulay, and William Stevens, *The Leisure Hour* Vol. 4 (Charleston, S.C.: Nabu Press, 1855).

14. "Benjamin Franklin: First American Diplomat," 1776–1785; 1776–1783; Milestones, Office of the Historian, https://history.state.gov/milestones/1776-1783/b-franklin.

15. Ibid.

16. Alix Browne, "Embassy Suite," *T Magazine,* Embassy Suite Comments, April 29, 2011.

17. Linda Grasso, "U.S. Ambassador to France and Wife Embark on a Once-in-a-Lifetime Adventure," *Huffington Post,* December 10, 2010.

18. Sarah-Eva Carlson, "Lincoln and the McCormick-Manny Case," February 1, 1995, http://www.lib.niu.edu/1995/ihy950230.html, accessed April 5, 2015.

19. Ibid.

20. Doris Kearns Goodwin, *Team of Rivals: The Political Genius of Abraham Lincoln* (New York: Simon & Schuster, 2005).

21. Ibid.

22. Michael Burlingame, *Abraham Lincoln: A Life* (Baltimore: Johns Hopkins University Press, 2008).

23. Tom Freiling, *Walking with Lincoln: Spiritual Strength from America's Favorite President* (Grand Rapids, MI: Revell, 2009).

Chapter 2: The Perks of Being in Power

1. Russ Choma, "Millionaires' Club: For First Time, Most Lawmakers Are Worth $1 Million-Plus," OpenSecrets RSS, January 9, 2014.

2. Rich McManus, "Collins Hosts Town Hall on Effects of Shutdown on NIH," *NIH Record,* November 8, 2013.

3. U.S. Congress, House of Representatives, Committee on Ethics, Member/Officer Post-Travel Disclosure Form: Rep. Sheila Jackson Lee, June 19, 2013, http://clerk.house.gov/GTImages/MT/2013/500009947.pdf.

4. U.S. Congress, House of Representatives, Committee on Ethics, Member/Officer Post-Travel Disclosure Form: Rep. Ruben Hinojosa, June 20, 2013, http://clerk.house.gov/GTImages/MT/2013/500009947.pdf.

5. Jonathan Tamari, "Congress' Ethics Office Strongly Questions Andrews' Spending," Philly.com, September 1, 2012.

6. U.S. Congress, House of Representatives, 2012 Financial Disclosure Statement: Rep. Joyce Beatty, May 15, 2013, http://clerk.house.gov/public_disc/financial-pdfs/2013/8211967.pdf.

7. Shane Goldmacher, "Nearly One in Five Members of Congress Gets Paid Twice," *National Journal*, June 27, 2013.

8. Ibid.

9. Bernice Napach, "Retirement Crisis: Over One-third of Americans Haven't Saved a Penny," *Yahoo Finance,* August 18, 2014.

10. Carl Campanile, "Rep. Nita Lowey Collects an Extra $10G Pension on Top of Her Salary," *New York Post,* September 17, 2012.

11. Dan Friedman, "Millionaires Dominate Congress, but NY Members Poorer," *NY Daily News,* January 9, 2014.

12. Courtney Subramanian, "GSA Scandal: So What Does $823,000 Buy You in Las Vegas?," *Time,* April 18, 2012.

13. Susan Davis, "IRS Employee Conferences Cost Taxpayers $49 Million," *USA Today,* June 4, 2013, http://www.usatoday.com/story/news/politics/2013/06/04/irs-audit-conferences-cost-taxpayers-millions/2388261/.

14. Susan Ferrechio, "IRS: $17k for Artist to Paint Portraits of Michael Jordan, Bono," *Washington Examiner,* June 4, 2013.

15. Jonathan Allen, "Hillary Clinton Faces Scrutiny for Use of Private Jets," Bloomberg.com, January 29, 2015.

16. Ida A. Brudnick, *Congressional Salaries and Allowances: In Brief* (CRS Report No. RL30064; Washington, DC: Congressional Research Service, 2014), http://library.clerk.house.gov/reference-files/114_20150106_Salary.pdf.

17. Ibid.

18. Donovan Slack and Paul Singer, "Senators Spent $1 Million on Charter Flights Last Year," *USA Today,* July 31, 2014.

19. Ryan Block, "Comcastic service disconnection," Soundcloud, 2015, https://soundcloud.com/ryan-block-10/comcastic-service.

20. "Congratulations to Comcast, Your 2014 Worst Company in America!," *Consumerist,* April 8, 2014.

21. Luke Mullins, "Comcast Kept Lists of VIP Customers but Says They Didn't Get Special Treatment," *Washingtonian,* January 8, 2015.

22. Luke Mullins, "How David Gregory Lost His Job," *Washingtonian,* December 21, 2014.

23. Douglas Ernst, "Money Talks: Every Senator Probing Time Warner Cable Merger Took Comcast PAC Cash," *Washington Times,* April 11, 2011.

24. Tony Romm, "Comcast Spreads Cash Wide on Hill," Politico, March 9, 2014.

25. David Martosko, "Obama Will Burn More than 35,000 Gallons of Fuel on Earth Day, Emitting 375 TONS of Carbon Dioxide," *Mail Online,* April 22, 2014.

Chapter 3. Do as We Say, Not as We Do

1. Richard Rubin, "Wealthy Clintons Use Trusts to Limit Estate Tax They Back," Bloomberg.com, June 17, 2014.

2. Ibid.

3. "Council for American Private Education," CAPE, http://www.capenet .org/facts.html, accessed January 14, 2015.

4. Lindsey Burke, "How Members of the 111th Congress Practice Private School Choice," Heritage Foundation, April 20, 2009.

5. Steve Peoples, "AP Sues State Department, Seeking Access to Clinton Records," Associated Press, March 11, 2015.

6. Colin Reed, "America Rising Submits FOIA Request For Clinton State Department Emails," *America Rising,* March 3, 2015, https://www .americarisingpac.org/america-rising-submits-foia-request-for-clinton -state-department-emails.

7. Robert Kennedy, "An Ill Wind Off Cape Cod," *New York Times*, December 15, 2005, http://www.nytimes.com/2005/12/16/opinion/ 16kennedy.html?_r=0.

8. Jennifer Fermino, "Big Blow to Kennedys," *New York Post*, April 29, 2010.

9. Jim Acosta, "After Criticizing White House over Unaccompanied Minors, Martin O'Malley Said Don't Send Them to Maryland Site," CNN, PoliticalTicker blog, July 15, 2014.

10. David Freedlander, *Daily Beast,* October 30, 2014.

11. Keith Phaneuf, "CT Declines to House Migrant Children at Southbury," *CT Mirror*, July 15, 2014.

12. Lisa Bartley, "Investigation: Serial Plaintiff Alfredo Garcia Who Filed 800 Lawsuits in LA Deported to Mexico," ABC7 Los Angeles, August 14, 2014.

13. Emma Dumain, "Capitol Violates Disabilities Law," *Roll Call*, October 18, 2012.

14. "'60 Minutes' Uncovers Pelosi's Insider Stock Trades," *Newsmax,* November 13, 2011, http://www.newsmax.com/InsideCover/pelosi-stock -insider-60minutes/2011/11/13/id/417848/.

15. John Carney, "Dick Durbin Sold Stocks into September 2008 Financial Panic," *Business Insider,* June 15, 2009.

16. "Report: US Lawmakers 18 Times Wealthier Than Average American," *Newsmax,* January 13, 2015.

17. Ylan Mui, "Americans Saw Wealth Plummet 40 percent from 2007 to 2010, Federal Reserve Says," *Washington Post,* June 11, 2012.

18. Tami Luhby, "Congress Is Getting Richer," CNNMoney, January 12, 2015.

Chapter 4. Life After Service

1. Laura Myers, "High Fashion, Expense for Hillary Travel," *Las Vegas Review-Journal*, August 16, 2014, http://www.reviewjournal.com/news/las-vegas/high-fashion-expense-hillary-travel.

2. Ibid.

3. David Knowles, "Hillary Clinton's Speech Demands: Lemons, Hummus, $300,000," Bloomberg.com. November 30, 2014, http://www.bloomberg.com/politics/articles/2014-11-30/hillary-clintons-speech-demands-lemons-hummus-300000.

4. Ibid.

5. Ibid.

6. Philip Rucker, "Plans for $300,000 UCLA Visit Give Rare Glimpse into Hillary Clinton's Paid Speaking Career," *Washington Post*, November 26, 2014, https://www.washingtonpost.com/politics/plans-for-ucla-visit-give-rare-glimpse-into-hillary-clintons-paid-speaking-career/2014/11/26/071eb0cc-7593-11e4-bd1b-03009bd3e984_story.html.

7. "Hillary Clinton Requires 'Presidential Suite,' Stenographer for Speaking Engagements, Report Says," Fox News, August 17, 2014, http://www.foxnews.com/politics/2014/08/17/hillary-clinton-requires-presidential-suite-for-speaking-engagements-report.html.

8. Rucker, "Plans for $300,000 UCLA Visit Give Rare Glimpse into Hillary Clinton's Paid Speaking Career."

9. Ibid.

10. Ibid.

11. Alexander Becker, "How the Clintons Went from 'Dead Broke' to Rich, with $104.9 Million for Ex-president's Speaking Fees," *Washington Post*, June 26, 2014, https://www.washingtonpost.com/politics/how-the-clintons-went-from-dead-broke-to-rich-bill-earned-1049-million-for-speeches/2014/06/26/8fa0b372-fd3a-11e3-8176-f2c941cf35f1_story.html.

12. Katherine Clarke, "The Clintons' Summer Home Is on the Market for $32.5M," *New York Daily News*, August 26, 2015, http://www

.nydailynews.com/life-style/real-estate/clintons-summer-home
-market-32-5m-article-1.2337988.

13. "Clintons Rent New $200K Hamptons Home after Cash Dispute with
    Regular Beach Getaway–but Still Fear They Could Be Spied on from
    Nearby Property," PageSix.com, August 14, 2013, http://pagesix.com/
    2013/08/14/clintons-rent-new-200k-hamptons-home-after-cash
    -dispute-with-regular-beach-getaway-but-still-fear-they-could-be
    -spied-on-from-nearby-property/.

14. "Government Spent Nearly $3.7M on Ex-presidents in 2012," Fox News,
    March 25, 2013, http://www.foxnews.com/politics/2013/03/25/
    government-spent-nearly-37m-on-ex-presidents-in-2012.html.

15. Wendy Ginsberg, "Former Presidents: Pensions, Office Allowances,
    and Other Federal Benefits," Congressional Research Service, May 25,
    2015, https://fas.org/sgp/crs/misc/RL34631.pdf.

16. Kia Makarechi, "Chelsea Clinton Quits NBC, Says Goodbye to
    $600,000 Salary," *Vanity Fair,* August 29, 2014, http://www.vanityfair
    .com/news/politics/2014/08/chelsea-clinton-quits-nbc.

17. Annie Karni, "Chelsea Clinton Paid up to $75K for Speeches," *New
    York Daily News,* July 10, 2014, http://www.nydailynews.com/news/
    politics/chelsea-clinton-paid-75k-speeches-article-1.1860261.

18. Sarah Stodola, "Chelsea Clinton Wedding: The Extravagance and
    the Price Tag," *Fiscal Times,* July 31, 2010, http://www.thefiscal
    times.com/Articles/2010/07/31/Chelsea-Clinton-Wedding-The
    -Extravagance-and-the-Price-Tag.

19. Dianna Marder, "Chelsea's Wedding Cake, a Gluten-free Masterpiece,"
    Philly.com archives, August 5, 2010, http://articles.philly.com/2010
    -08-05/food/24971387_1_gluten-free-wedding-cake-pastry.

20. Philip Caulfield, "Chelsea Clinton to Buy $10.5 Million Apartment,"
    New York Daily News, March 14, 2014, http://www.nydailynews
    .com/life-style/real-estate/chelsea-clinton-buys-10-5-million-article
    -1.1288710.

21. Ted Johnson, "MPAA Chairman Chris Dodd's Compensation Was
    $3.3 Million in 2012," *Variety,* November 19, 2013, http://variety.com/
    2013/biz/news/chris-dodd-salary-2012-1200837496/.

22. Rob Hotakainen, "A $130,500 Pension? Some in Congress Say No, but
    Most Cash In," McClatchyDC, October 1, 2013, http://www.mcclatchydc
    .com/news/politics-government/congress/article24776752.html.

23. Catalina Camia, "Pension, Benefits for Anthony Weiner Could Top
    $1M," *USA Today,* June 17, 2011, http://content.usatoday.com/
    communities/onpolitics/post/2011/06/anthony-weiner-resignation
    -pension-campaign-funds/1#.Vpe-NLxViko.

24. Becket Adams, "15 of the Most Bizarre Purchases Jesse Jackson Jr. Made with Embezzled Campaign Cash," *The Blaze,* February 21, 2013, http://www.theblaze.com/stories/2013/02/21/15-of-the-most -bizarre-things-jesse-jackson-jr-bought-with-embezzled-campaign -cash/.

25. Chuck Goudie, "Jesse Jackson Jr. Still Eligible for Government Pension, Disability Pay," ABC7 Chicago, August 4, 2013, http://abc7chicago .com/archive/9206552/.

26. Michael Luo, "In Banking, Emanuel Made Money and Connections," *New York Times,* December 3, 2008, http://www.nytimes.com/2008/ 12/04/us/politics/04emanuel.html?_r=0.

27. Tarini Parti, "Gibbs, Messina, Plouffe's Energy Trip," Politico, May 30, 2013, http://www.politico.com/story/2013/05/robert-gibbs-jim -messina-david-plouffe-azerbaijan-trip-092054.

Chapter 5. Family Affairs

1. Chuck Neubauer, "In Nevada, the Name to Know Is Reid," *Los Angeles Times,* June 23, 2003, http://articles.latimes.com/2003/jun/23/ nation/na-sons23.

2. Ibid.

3. "What's Next After Family Affair?," CREW Blog, March 28, 2012, http://www.citizensforethics.org/blog/entry/whats-next-after-family -affair.

4. Jane Ann Morrison, "Shift in Henderson City Attorney Qualifications a Boon for Josh Reid," *Las Vegas Review-Journal,* November 21, 2011, http://www.reviewjournal.com/jane-ann-morrison/shift-henderson -city-attorney-qualifications-boon-josh-reid.

5. Ibid.

6. Ibid.

7. Ibid.

8. Geoff Earle, "Reid Campaign Cash Paid to Granddaughter Hits $31,000," *New York Post,* March 28, 2014, http://nypost.com/2014/ 03/28/reid-campaign-cash-paid-to-granddaughter-hits-31000/.

9. Paul Sonne, "Biden's Son, Kerry Family Friend Join Ukrainian Gas Producer's Board," *Wall Street Journal,* May 13, 2014, http://www.wsj .com/articles/SB10001424052702303851804579560542284706288.

10. Byron York, "The Senator from MBNA," *National Review Online,* August 23, 2008, http://www.nationalreview.com/article/225417/senator -mbna-byron-york.

11. James V. Grimaldi, "Obama, Biden's Son Linked by Earmarks," *Washington Post,* August 27, 2008, http://www.washingtonpost.com/wp -dyn/content/article/2008/08/26/AR2008082603894.html.

12. Ibid.

13. Stephen Braun, "Biden's Son Faces No Bar Review after Discharge," WLUK-TV, Green Bay, October 17, 2014, http://fox11online.com/ news/nation-world/bidens-son-faces-no-bar-review-after-discharge.

14. Lachlan Markay, "Pelosi Subsidies Benefit Husband's Investment in Dem Mega-Donor's Company," *Washington Free Beacon,* August 15, 2014, http://freebeacon.com/politics/pelosi-subsidies-benefit -husbands-investment-in-dem-mega-donors-company/.

15. Ibid.

16. Sharyl Atkisson, "ATF Fast and Furious: New Documents Show Attorney General Eric Holder Was Briefed in July 2010," CBS News, October 3, 2011, http://www.cbsnews.com/news/atf-fast-and-furious -new-documents-show-attorney-general-eric-holder-was-briefed-in-july -2010/.

17. Cheryl Chumley, "Eric Holder's Wife Wins 'Executive Privilege' for 'Fast and Furious,' Watchdog Says," *Washington Times,* October 24, 2014, http://www.washingtontimes.com/news/2014/oct/24/eric -holders-wife-wins-executive-privilege-for-fas/.

18. Alex Johnson, "Russert's Son Joins NBC News as Correspondent," Today.com, July 31, 2008, http://www.today.com/id/25935768/ns/ today-today_news/t/russerts-son-joins-nbc-news-correspondent/.

19. "Luke Russert Getting $500K to Be on 'Meet the Press,'" *New York Post,* Page Six, September 10, 2014, http://pagesix.com/2014/09/10/ luke-russert-getting-500k-to-be-on-meet-the-press/.

20. "WVU Needs Impartial Inquiry into Manchin Daughter's Degree," *Herald Dispatch,* December 29, 2007, http://www.herald-dispatch .com/opinion/editorial-wvu-needs-impartial-inquiry-into-manchin -daughter-s-degree/article_b0407f18-b6d7-5746-a0fc-11b6da934f40 .html.

21. "Review of Conduct by a High-Ranking Official in the Hiring of a Trademark Organization Employee," U.S. Patent and Trademark Office, July 8, 2014, https://www.oig.doc.gov/oigpublications/13-0726 _unredacted.pdf.

22. Ibid.

23. Rob Copeland, "Hedge Fund Co-Founded by Chelsea Clinton's Husband Suffers Losses Tied to Greece," *Wall Street Journal,* February 3, 2015, http://www.wsj.com/articles/hedge-fund-co-founded-by-chelsea -clintons-husband-suffers-losses-tied-to-greece-1423000325.

24. Ibid.

25. Andrew Stiles, "Don't Give Your Money to Clinton Son-in-Law Marc Mezvinsky," *Washington Free Beacon,* February 4, 2015, http://freebeacon.com/blog/dont-give-your-money-to-clinton-son-in-law -marc-mezvinsky/.

26. Carl Hulse and Ashley Parker, "John Dingell to Retire After Nearly 60 Years in House," *New York Times,* February 24, 2014, http://www .nytimes.com/2014/02/25/us/politics/dingell-to-retire-from-congress .html.

27. Paul C. Nagel, *John Quincy Adams: A Public Life, a Private Life* (New York: Knopf, 1997).

Chapter 6. Narcissism: "Extreme Selfishness, with a Grandiose View of One's Own Talkers and a Craving for Admiration"

1. "Definition of Narcissism in English," Definition of Narcissism in Oxford Dictionary, http://www.oxforddictionaries.com/us/definition/ american_english/narcissism.

2. Jonathan Strong, "Congressional Bosses from Hell: Sheila Jackson Lee," *Daily Caller,* March 2, 2011, http://dailycaller.com/2011/03/02/ congressional-bosses-from-hell-sheila-jackson-lee/.

3. Ibid.

4. Ibid.

5. Ibid.

6. Catalina Camia, "How Rep. Engel Came to Be State of the Union's 'Aisle Hog,'" *USA Today,* OnPolitics, January 20, 2015, http://onpolitics .usatoday.com/2015/01/20/eliot-engel-sotu-aisle-hog/.

7. Ibid.

8. "Rep. Engel: Obama Didn't Snub Me!," NBC News, February 13, 2013, http://usnews.nbcnews.com/_news/2013/02/13/16952245-rep-engel -obama-didnt-snub-me?lite.

9. Judy Kurtz, "Reid's 'Lincoln' Senate Screening Request: Popcorn," *The Hill,* December 7, 2012, http://thehill.com/blogs/in-the-know/in-the -know/271695-reids-lincoln-senate-screening-request-popcorn.

10. Roxanne Roberts, "Sally Quinn Throws Ben Bradlee One Last A-list Party," *Washington Post,* October 29, 2014, https://www.washingtonpost .com/lifestyle/style/sally-quinn-throws-ben-bradlee-one-last-a-list -party/2014/10/29/76323b46-5fa9-11e4-91f7-5d89b5e8c251_story .html.

11. Richard Vetterli and Gary C. Bryner, *In Search of the Republic: Public Virtue and the Roots of American Government* (Totowa, NJ: Rowman & Littlefield, 1987).

Chapter 7. Politicos and the Press: A Love Story

1. Michael Calderone, "JournoList: Inside the Echo Chamber," Politico, March 17, 2009, http://www.politico.com/story/2009/03/journolist -inside-the-echo-chamber-020086.

2. Jonathan Strong, "Documents Show Media Plotting to Kill Stories about Rev. Jeremiah Wright," *Daily Caller,* July 20, 2010, http:// dailycaller.com/2010/07/20/documents-show-media-plotting-to-kill -stories-about-rev-jeremiah-wright/.

3. Ibid.

4. Ibid.

5. Ibid.

6. Jonathan Stein, "In Open Letter, Journalists Slam ABC Debate," *Mother Jones,* April 18, 2008, http://www.motherjones.com/mojo/ 2008/04/open-letter-journalists-slam-abc-debate.

7. Patrick Howley, "White House Holds Obamacare Background Briefing with Liberal Reporters," *Daily Caller,* July 12, 2013, http://dailycaller .com/2013/07/12/white-house-holds-obamacare-background-briefing -with-liberal-reporters/.

8. "Juan Williams Meets Privately With Obama: 'They're in Full Fight Mode,'" *Fox News Insider,* November 21, 2013, http://insider.foxnews .com/2013/11/21/obama-meets-privately-juan-williams-other-liberal -journalists-white-house-obamacare.

9. Paul Bedard, "Elections Over, Obama Turns to Racial Divide," *Washington Examiner,* February 2, 2015, http://www.washingtonexaminer .com/elections-over-obama-turns-to-racial-divide/article/2559649.

10. Dylan Byers, "Stengel Leaving Time for State Dept," Politico, September 12, 2013, http://www.politico.com/story/2013/09/richard-stengel -leaving-time-state-department-096732.

11. Elspeth Reeve, "Rick Stengel Is at Least the 24th Journalist to Work for the Obama Administration," *The Wire,* September 12, 2013, http:// www.thewire.com/politics/2013/09/rick-stengel-least-24-journalist -go-work-obama-administration/69362/.

12. "Amendment I (Speech and Press): Thomas Jefferson to Edward Carrington," January 16, 1787, http://press-pubs.uchicago.edu/founders/ documents/amendI_speechs8.html.

Chapter 8. The American Family Business

1. Richard Berke, "U.S. Attorney in Miami to Take No Active Role in the Noriega Trial," *New York Times,* January 13, 1990.

2. Ken Cummins, "Bush to Nominate Dexter Lehtinen As Top Prosecutor," *Sun Sentinel,* March 1, 1990.

3. Amy Stromberg, "Lehtinen Temper Subject of Report," *Sun Sentinel,* January 20, 1990.

4. Jim McGee, "Between Politics and Professionalism: One Prosecutor's Tenure and Tactics," *Washington Post,* January 14, 1993.

5. Ibid.

6. Sean Davis, "The U.S. Constitution Actually Bans Hillary's Foreign Gov't. Payola," *Federalist,* March 2, 2015.

7. Ibid.

Chapter 9. All the President's Money Men: Or, How to Be an Ambassador Without Really Trying

1. The U.S. Ambassador Residence, Winfield House, http://london.usembassy.gov/rcwinfld.html.

2. The U.S. Ambassador Residence, Villa Taverna, http://italy.usembassy.gov/ambassador/residence.html.

3. J. J. Martin, "Susan Tolson: An American in Paris," *Harper's Bazaar,* March 25, 2011.

4. Ibid.

5. Alix Browne, "Embassy Suite," *T Magazine,* Embassy Suite Comments, April 29, 2011.

6. Mary Bruce, "What Does It Cost to Be an Obama Ambassador?," ABC News, February 7, 2014.

7. Ibid.

8. Juliet Eilperin, "From Donors to Diplomats: How Nominating Political Allies Has Handed Obama a New Problem," *Washington Post,* February 14, 2014.

9. Ibid.

10. Lisa Lerer, "Obama Ambassadors Gave $13.6 Million in Campaign Money," Bloomberg.com, July 25, 2013, accessed January 14, 2016.

11. J. W. Fedderke and D. Jett, "What Price the Court of St. James?: Political Influences on Ambassadorial Postings of the United States of America," Economic Research Southern Africa, 2011.

12. Ibid.

13. "Obama's Top Fund-Raisers," *New York Times,* September 12, 2012.

14. Joshua Keating, "Do Ambassadors Actually Have to Know Stuff About the Countries They're Sent To?," *Slate,* January 23, 2014.

15. "Future US Envoy Displays Total Ignorance of Norway," *Local,* January 23, 2014, http://www.thelocal.no/20140123/next-us-ambassador.

16. Chris Zubak-Skees, "See the Ambassadorships Big Money Can Bring," Center for Public Integrity, September 19, 2013.

17. Ibid.

18. Office of Inspections, 2012, https://oig.state.gov/system/files/184725 .pdf.

19. Ibid.

20. Ibid.

21. "Obama's New Ambassador Nominees Gave Big—and Bundled Bigger," OpenSecrets RSS, June 18, 2009, http://www.opensecrets.org/news/ 2009/06/obamas-new-ambassador-nominees/.

22. Menachem Gantz, " 'Jew-Hate Stems from Conflict,' " *Ynet,* December 3, 2011.

23. Ibid.

24. Michael Beckel, "Democratic Financier Cynthia Stroum Flames Out After Brief Stint as Barack Obama's Ambassador to Luxembourg," OpenSecrets RSS, February 4, 2011.

25. "Report of Inspection," Embassy Luxembourg, Luxembourg, 2011, https://oig.state.gov/system/files/156129.pdf.

26. Ibid.

27. Ibid.

28. Ibid.

29. Frank James, "U.S. Ambassador Exits Europe Post Before Scathing Report About Her," NPR, February 4, 2011.

30. "Report of Inspection," Embassy Luxembourg.

31. Ibid.

32. Noel Brinkerhoff, "Ambassador to Luxembourg: Who Is Robert Mandell?," *AllGov,* August 6, 2011.

33. Eugene Kiely, "Benghazi Timeline," *FactCheck,* October 26, 2012.

34. "Accountability Review Board," U.S. State Department, http://www .state.gov/documents/organization/202446.pdf.

35. Ibid.

36. "Hearing on Benghazi: Exposing Failure and Recognizing Courage," Committee on Oversight & Government Reform, May 8, 2013, http://oversight.house.gov/wp-content/uploads/2013/05/Nordstrom -Testimony-5-8-Benghazi-COMPLETE1.pdf.

37. "Increased Cost of Building 'Design Excellence' U.S. Embassies," CBS News, June 4, 2014.

38. Mark Landler, "Obama Nominates Caroline Kennedy to Be Ambassador to Japan," *New York Times,* July 24, 2013.

Chapter 10. Taking Back Our Country

1. George McGovern, "George McGovern in the Journal," *Wall Street Journal,* October 12, 2012.

2. Ibid.

3. Ibid.

4. Ibid.

5. John H. Fund, "Term Limitation: An Idea Whose Time Has Come," Cato Institute, October 30, 1990.

6. Edward H. Crane and Roger Pilon, eds., *The Politics and Law of Term Limits* (Washington, DC: Cato Institute, 1994).

7. James Madison and Robert J. Brugger, *The Papers of James Madison* (Charlottesville: University Press of Virginia, 1986).

8. Peter Schweizer, *Throw Them All Out: How Politicians and Their Friends Get Rich Off Insider Stock Tips, Land Deals, and Cronyism That Would Send the Rest of Us to Prison* (Boston: Houghton Mifflin Harcourt, 2011).

9. Melanie Hicken, "Will Your Congressman Retire Richer than You?," CNNMoney, July 30, 2013.

10. Ibid.

11. Stephen Losey, "Federal Pension Systems' Unfunded Liabilities Sky-rocket," *Federal Times,* February 20, 2013.

12. Ibid.

13. Benjamin Franklin, "Dangers of a Salaried Bureaucracy," Lecture, Constitutional Convention of 1787, Philadelphia, January 1, 1787.

14. Randy Hultgren, "How to Fix the Broken Budget," CNBC, May 6, 2015.

15. Gregory Korte, "U.S. Has 42 Programs to Help You Get to the Doctor," *USA Today*, April 15, 2015.

16. "GAO's Duplication Report Reveals Mountain of Federal Mismanagement," Citizens Against Government Waste, April 14, 2015.

17. Clyde Wayne Crews Jr., "Ten Thousand Commandments," Annual Snapshot of the Federal Regulatory State, May 1, 2015.

18. Josh Zumbrun, "The Federal Government Now Employs the Fewest People Since 1966," Real Time Economics RSS, November 7, 2014.

19. Zeke Miller, "Meet the Man Who Has 279 Members of Congress in His Pocket," *Business Insider,* November 21, 2011.

20. Byron Tau, "White House: Biden, Obama Unaware of Security Requests," Politico 44 blog, October 12, 2012.

21. David Martosko, "White House Says Obama Only Learned of VA Wait-List Scandal on TV (Just Like the IRS, Fast and Furious and Reporter Snooping Scandals)," *Mail Online,* May 19, 2014.

22. Greg Botelho, "Sebelius: President Didn't Know of Obamacare Website's Woes in Advance," CNNPolitics.com, October 23, 2013.

23. "President Obama Says He Was Unaware of IRS Targeting Before Scandal Broke," CBS New York, May 16, 2013.

INDEX

Page numbers in *italics* refer to illustrations.

ABOUT THE AUTHOR

Michelle Fields is a political reporter who has held positions at Fox News, Breitbart, PJ Media, and the Daily Caller. In addition to her reporting work, Michelle has appeared on C-SPAN, CNBC, Sky News, and various programs on the Fox News Channel and Fox Business Network.